For We Are More Than Conquerors

LUKE SOTO

Trilogy Christian Publishers

A Wholly Owned Subsidary of Trinity Broadcasting Network
2442 Michelle Drive
Tustin, CA 92780

For information, address Trilogy Christian Publishing Rights Department, 2442 Michelle Drive, Tustin, Ca 92780.

Trilogy Christian Publishing/ TBN and colophon are trademarks of Trinity Broadcasting Network.

For information about special discounts for bulk purchases, please contact Trilogy Christian Publishing.
Manufactured in the United States of America

10 9 8 7 6 5 4 3 2 1
Library of Congress Cataloging-in-Publication Data is avai-la-ble.
ISBN 978-1-64773-218-9
ISBN 978-1-64773-219-6 (ebook)

Dedication

I dedicate this book to:

Our Lady of Victory, Our Lady of Perpetual Help, Our Lady Undoer of Knots.

To the Holy Ghost, which is the true conquering Spirit: I never would have made it without You; we go and move on together; You lead me. My buddy in arms, You fought off those devils.

To Jesus Christ, my Brother: thank You for Your sacrifice; You went through hell so I don't have to, that I may be saved.

To God the Father: thank You for saving me and my family; You have made me your son. I love You for Your care and correction; thanks, Dad.

To the Lion of Judah: thanks for roaring over me and my family. You took us into your pride and roared over my life.

And to the Holy Family: Thanks for the sacrifice You made for our salvation.

To my family: I love you guys; we've gone through a lot.

Contents

I completed *For We Are More Than Conquerors* on September 23, 2006. I started it on January 1, 2006.

May the Holy Ghost haunt you.
May the fire of the Lord burn within you with such
passion and love that all around you are consumed.
May God spring forth from your life and show you
your surroundings, and may His presence rise up in
you and show forth the glory of God.
May the Holy Ghost revive the Spirit of praise and
worship, and may the glory of God shine forth and
bring God glory by the readers' lives.

Rise up, O Lion of Judah, and roar for the remnant
that remains and cannot go forth without Your
guidance. Rise up, O glory of God, and let Your
light shine through the darkness and cut through the
night, and show forth Your eternal light that the glory of God be praised, and the Spirit of deliverance
and repentance break forth through the dry, parched
land, and healing take place by Your light.
May the Spirit of healing and wholeness run through
the streets of Your believers. May Your Spirit of
repentance rise up and burn within us, and grant us
forgiveness. Forget revival, Lord; grant us repentance, grant us love, grant us Your saving grace and
allow us to draw near to You.
May You always hear the voice of the believer who
bares his heart and soul to You. May Your divine
love and passion rise up in us and bear forth the
fruit of Your true Spirit. May the glory of the Lord
rise up and bring us to Your eternal love. May Your
redemption wash over us and break the chains of
bondage and allow us repentance. Rise up, O Lord,

and save us, Your people.

May the hand of the Lord be upon you and break every dam made by the devil, and every demonic spirit looking to keep us in oppression.

Holy Spirit of the LORD of Hosts, break free Your anointing, and may You, Holy Ghost, bring forth true repentance and healing and deliverance to all who believe. Rise up and bring us into Your love; break that spirit of fear and death that holds us under oppression.

Lord, I say like St. Patrick:

I arise today
Through the strength of heaven;
Light of the sun,
Splendor of fire,
Speed of lightning,
Swiftness of the wind,
Depth of the sea,
Stability of the earth,
Firmness of the rock.

I arise today
Through God's strength to pilot me;
God's might to uphold me,
God's wisdom to guide me,

God's eye to look before me,
God's ear to hear me,
God's word to speak for me,
God's hand to guard me,
God's way to lie before me
, God's shield to protect me,
God's hosts to save me Afar and anear,
Alone or in a multitude.

Christ shield me today
Against wounding
Christ with me, Christ before me, Christ behind me,
Christ in me, Christ beneath me, Christ above me,
Christ on my right, Christ on my left,
Christ when I lie down, Christ when I sit down,
Christ in the heart of everyone who thinks of me,
Christ in the mouth of everyone who speaks of me,
Christ in the eye that sees me,
Christ in the ear that hears me.
I arise today
Through the mighty strength
Of the Lord of creation.
Oh, Spirit of the Lord, rise up, and by Your blood
break every evil chain of demonic oppression in our
lives, and roar with such a roar that the demonic op-
pression and the demonic possession must flee back
to the pit of hell that they came from. Holy Enforcer
of the Word, rise up and save us, Your people. May
Your bell ring for freedom to the captives and liberty
to the oppressed. Holy Ghost, show us and help us
to live the life that was supposed to be lived by the

glory of God. Let Your Holy Ghost fire burn down the evil, the sin, the darkness, and strengthen our hands to the work that lies before us.

By the holy blood of Jesus that flows from Calvary for the forgiveness of sins and the ability to think like a free man in Christ, I pray that You hear my prayer, the prayer of Your faithful, and deliver us from evil. In the name of Jesus Christ, I declare: be free by Your very Word, Lord.

In the name of Jesus Christ, I pray.

Amen!
Let all those who stand in agreement pray this with me and expect an answer from God.

May the Holy Ghost haunt you, the reader, and raise up the spirit of a conqueror in Jesus Christ our Lord for His glory. May God rise up in you, and may you live the life that Christ has for you.

May the hand of the Lord be upon you,

and may you follow God all the days of your life.

Preface

I wrote this book because I thought this was a preaching, but it was not. It was a teaching. A teaching from Christ that would revolutionize my life from here on forward. The question was a hook that took me on a journey.

I grew up in church hearing that we are more than conquerors, and then heard the rest of the conversation. But God tapped on my shoulder and then asked me, "What does it mean to be more than a conqueror?" I honestly never thought to ask or think that. Then He said, "Exactly. Why not talk about it?" So, I did—or so I thought. It actually went the other way around: He did, and I listened. I had the Holy Ghost come on me and start to teach me what it was to go and to live this out.

It was a living out of the sermons. "Be the living example of what you preach," is what He was teaching me. I never felt so much pain and conflict in my life. I still don't know, but it's a heck of a journey that I hope God continues to lead me on. It's a life that I have not seen any Christian, to date, live.

The examples that I have seen have been those of the past generations, and He shows me that it is possible if it is applied not just for the church building. He shows me the lives of the past preachers and teachers. Rev. Shambach, GK Chesterton, Smith Wigglesworth, Amy Semple-McPherson, TL Lowry, AA Allen, Benny Hinn, Katherine Kuhlmann,

Billy Sunday, Billy Graham, William J. Seymour, Lester Sumrall, Charles Finney, the "What Would Jesus Do" movement of the 1890's, led by Charles Sheldon, Charles Parham, Evan Roberts, Jonathan Edwards, and that one black railroad preacher from the 1800s whose name I believe was Cotton Mather (forgive me, sir, if I am mistaken)—all these and more. Since God has made me a Catholic, I can say that even more so from the beginning of church history, the saints glorified God with a life that revolutionized the world around them. But all remain the same—ordinary people, who gave themselves over to God for Him to do with as He saw fit. And so, the Spirit that conquered the land of evil and death is the same Spirit that looks to reside and move in the lives of those of us of this age to go forth and glorify God by our lives.

And we can do this why, you may ask?

-Luke Soto

FOR WE ARE MORE THAN CONQUERORS

Definiton of being a Conqueror

In the Merriam-Webster Dictionary, the word *conquer* means:

Conquer:

1) to gain or acquire by force of arms: subjugate

2) to overcome by force of arms: vanquish

3) to gain mastery over or win by overcoming obstacles or opposition

4) to overcome by mental power or moral power: surmount

Intransitive sense: to be victorious

So, what does this mean? It means that if we are more than conquerors, we have gained what we have by arming ourselves. We have acquired the land that God has for us by the force of our weapons; we have subjugated the enemy. What does *subjugate* mean,

1

then?

Subjugate:

1) to bring under control and governance as a subject

2) to make submissive

So, you mean to tell me that the land that we are a part of, we govern? That land, then, and the things that we have conquered in our warfare, is made submissive to us. That must mean that when we are faced with that problem in our lives, it must leave because of the level of our authority.

Now, Jesus vanquished the enemy, and Jesus is found in us that do believe in Him, so now we go through the motions of being tested—yeah, that's right—we already overcame the battle when Christ died and rose again.

So, we then vanquish the enemy from the land that Christ gave to us as our inheritance.

Well, what does it mean to *vanquish*?

Vanquish:

1) to overcome in battle: subdue completely

2) to defeat in a conflict or contest

3) to gain mastery over (an emotion, passion, or temptation)

So that means that as we go up higher in the Lord Jesus Christ, then we must do battle. And because we are already the victors, we still fight to beat down that thing in the present, so that in the future we don't have to deal with it anymore. Through the force of a battle—a conflict—we have beaten the enemy to the point that he has completely been subdued, and not one piece of that thing can move without us knowing it. So that emotion, that desire, that thing that holds you at a point of embarrassment must stop, for when you battle, you are determined to be the victor after that one battle. That is why you must pray without ceasing to keep continual communication open during the battle, for after that warfare takes place you will have annihilated that subject. So that is why the battle is so fierce. Because it's life or death, and that devil doesn't want to die; the thought process is, "It's either you or me, and it isn't going to be me," so those demons stick it to you as hard as they can. Now that we are more than conquerors, we have surmounted the enemy. What does it mean to *surmount*, if we have surmounted?

Surmount:

1) obsolete: to surpass in quality or attainment: excel 2) to prevail over: overcome 3) to get to the top of; climb 4) to stand or lie at the top of

Intransitive sense: to be victorious So that means, then, that we are men and women of worth, that we have some value to us that the devil doesn't have, and that the treasure in us has only been obtained by the battle that we came out of; that is what makes us "men and women of worth," of value. It's from the death counts to the demonic realm, and the victory that we gain by taking back our land. That also means that when we do reach the top of that hill that we had to climb—or the top of the mountain we climbed—we now have a strategic point that will help us to overcome the next obstacle in our lives. Thus, this is the testimony that believers in Jesus Christ have. We fight the battle, vanquish the enemy, and finally reach the top and have a value to God that the enemy can't have. That's why we have such a hard time getting to our breakthrough, because the devil thinks, "If I can make you feel tired, you'll never be that man or woman of worth, and then I am worth more than you will ever be." But if you can just pull through, then you have something that you would never have been able to have, never have been able to hear from a preaching, never have been able to get advice from, but for the climb that you had. Now, look at the word *lie*—it means to be located or situated somewhere; to occupy a certain position.

So then, the place that you reach when at the top is a place that is not only an expansion of your territory, but also a strategic place where the devil can't attack you—but you can plan an invasion to take back the land that the devil is occupying, where your borders end.

Thus, the prayer of Jabez takes place: "*Oh that you would enlarge my territory, and that your hand*

4

would be with me, that you would keep me from evil."

1 Chronicles 4:10 New King James Version (NKJV) *"And Jabez called on the God of Israel saying, 'Oh, that You would bless me indeed, and enlarge my territory, that Your hand would be with me, and that You would keep me from evil, that I may not cause pain!' So God granted him what he requested."*

And the Lord granted him his request. That, my friend, is the most powerful prayer that any person who has allowed God to season them can pray. And it will be granted to them, for that is a spiritual warfare prayer. To take back the land the devil has taken over, to reset the boundaries back to the place where they need to be—oh, you think it's the land. But I tell you it's not, it is the church. You sometimes hear that the devil has infiltrated the church; well, let's set the church back up to the glory where it was intended to be.

Well, this thing—to be a conqueror—tells us to *subdue* the land, but how can we if we don't even know what the word means, and how to carry it out?

Subdue:

1) to conquer and bring into subjection: vanquish

2) to bring under control, especially by an exertion of the will: curb

3) to bring under cultivation

4) to reduce the intensity or degree of tone down

When we conquer a land, it means that we bring it under our subjection when we have vanquished the enemy. We now govern that land that belongs to us, and now it is controlled by our will; that is why Jesus said, *"Not my will, but yours be done."*

Luke 22:42 New King James Version (NKJV)
"Saying, 'Father, if it is Your will, take this cup away from Me; nevertheless not My will, but Yours, be done.'"

For if we are to cultivate that land with our will not matching up to God's, it will cause that land to be subjected to a level of chaos we have never known before. For no one can serve two masters; that's why the land begins to split—and instead of going out, the land starts to cave in, causing people to turn on each other because they are not under the will of God, but their own.

So now we can't go out and continue the battle, because of the death that happens behind us. Because we haven't asked to be restored to the rightful will of God and to see how He would govern these lands that we conquered; therefore, we conquer less and less, because God doesn't want us going out and making a bigger mess for Him to clean up later. In the meantime, while this stalling is taking place, the demonic realm takes back the land that we have just conquered, and overtakes those who are stuck and haven't committed to walk in the righteous will

6

of God; thus making backsliders, thus making hot Christians turn cold. But there is a remnant rising, taking back what rightfully belongs to God.

We have overcome the devil and his works by the blood of the Lamb, the Lord Jesus Christ; we, as conquerors, overcome.

Revelation 12:11 New King James Version (NKJV) *"And they overcame him by the blood of the Lamb and by the word of their testimony, and they did not love their lives to the death."*

Overcome:

to get the better of: surmount

Intransitive sense: to gain the superiority: win

"He got the better of me, but I'll get him back"— have you ever heard that? Well, that thing or person overcame you because you didn't have your guard up and weren't on alert; so, because of that, he became your superior—he won you over. You are now his, because you didn't watch your guard. But we have been bought back by the blood of the Lamb, the Lord Jesus Christ, so now we can overcome. And while you were away, allowing that thing free reign over your life, you can finally come back and say, "Get out in the name of Jesus; I have come to take my rightful place." And the devil that was your superior is no more; he must step down, because you have become the superior, taking authority where you belong—in your place.

So, now that we have become a person who over-
comes, who rules by submission, who wages a
warfare that leads to victory, who fights with the
weapons that were given to him—in all these aspects
of a conqueror, we excel; we are people who have
a high success. *Excel* sounds like a low or "of no
importance" word; well, the word *excel* means:

Excel:

to be superior, to surpass in accomplishment or
achievement

Intransitive sense: to be distinguishable by superiority: surpass others

Isn't that something—it's because you're a conquer-
or that that business is flourishing the way it is; the
only reason that hotel is booked is because there is
a believer in Christ that is staying there; the only
reason the office is staying ahead of schedule is because a believer in Christ is leading the project. This
is how the testimony of God is supposed to be—not
reversed around, and you can see this by the way the
people volunteer or work. If you're a Christian, the
bosses think twice because once you work and the
work starts backing up, or the sick rate increases,
this shows you that you're not walking right. You're
producing the opposite effect; it's because you're
walking around defeated and conquered by the devil.
If you would only stand up and fight, you would
overcome and win the battle and take your place
where God puts you. And all you have to do is to

submit to the will of God and watch Him bring you up high to the point where you prosper, where you conquer the land you walk on, in the name of Jesus. So rise, and become a conqueror in the Lord, for it will be in Him that He will set the steps that you are to walk.

In a sense, you're climbing up the mountain called your life; so, if we continue to walk in Christ then this is how to walk. We walk in the authority of Jesus Christ; we walk in the name of the Lord. So then, when we climb the mountain, we've got to know what it is to climb.

Climb:

1) a) to go upwards with gradual or continuous progress: rise, ascend; b) to increase gradually; c) to slope upward

2) a) to go upward or raise oneself, especially by grasping or clutching with the hands; b) of a plant, to ascend in growth (as by twining)

3) to go about or down, usually by grasping or holding with the hands (climb down the ladder)

4) to get into or out of clothing, usually with some haste or effort

Transitive sense: 1) to go upward on or along, to the top of, or over

2) to draw or pull oneself up, or to the top of, by using hands and feet

3) to grow up or over

When we climb the mountain, we are always going up; we don't descend. The movement is always an upward movement—it's there to bring you up to the next level of the mountain, where the air is thinner and a lot crisper and cleaner. The climb is always there to ascend to the heavens. Whether you move fast or slow, you're still going to get there, but you never leave the mountain. The climb up the mountain is a gradual one; you don't just fly up the mountain—it is a continual progress.

In order to climb the mountain, you don't just walk. In order to pull yourself up the mountain, you must grasp onto something with your hands. Now here is the kicker: the only way you can get up to the next part of the mountain is that you must cling to Jesus; the more you grasp ahold of Him, the higher you will be able to climb up the mountain. That's where your breakthrough comes; every time you are about to break out you get a tiredness in your mind, in your body, and in your hands, which represents your works. So the more work you do in yourself, with the Lord Jesus Christ you are climbing the mountain; you are going higher into Him, you are getting to know who you are; there is life in the tongue, power in the blood.

Now, if you never do any work or any movement, then you are not moving the way you should be moving. The word *climb* also introduces the word *plant*. Now, how can *plant* be a part of the climb? Well, the Tree of Life called Jesus Christ says that He is the true vine and we are the vine branches, and any branch that does not bear any fruit is cut off from Him and thrown into the fire.

Well, there you go—a vine must bear fruit in order to survive. When we climb a mountain, that means that God is always climbing and then we, too must always be climbing. To what? To perfection. To the glory of the Lord Jesus Christ, who died and rose again, who was placed in a tomb and was not found there after a three-day period.

The dictionary—according to the definition of the word *climb*—also states that the growth of a plant by ascending is called *twining*. Now *twining* means that the object is weaved in with another—to encircle, to tie together—in other words, when God plants us, we are planted next to Him. Throughout our lifetime, we get wrapped around the thing that is planted next to us—like a vine that you sometimes see wrapped around a pole or growing along a wall or on the wall. As time goes on, when you pull me you are also pulling the thing that is attached to me; so, no longer am I Luke, but I am the extension of Jesus' body, for He and I are the same. Like Galatians says, *"It is no longer I who live, but Christ lives in me."*

Galatians 2:20 New King James Version (NKJV)
"I have been crucified with Christ; it is no longer I who live, but Christ lives in me; and the life which I now live in the flesh I live by faith in the Son of God, who loved me and gave Himself for me."

The word *climb* also says to go about or down by holding or grasping with the hands. So now, if we are always to be moving up in Christ, the only thing that can hold us down is our flesh; so the more you hold onto your flesh and less onto God, then you are not ascending to the holy throne of God but descending into the pits of fire. That is why Peter said:

1 Peter 2:24 New King James Version (NKJV)
"Who Himself bore our sins in His own body on the tree, that we, having died to sins, might live for righteousness—by whose stripes you were healed."

For that day that you accepted Jesus Christ is the day that you dropped your flesh. You see, there was an exchange: His righteousness for your sin, His holiness for your darkness, His healing for your sickness, His love for your fear, His hope for your despondency, His salvation for your damnation, His sacrifice for your freedom—but here is the thing. You can pick up your flesh again, even after you accept Jesus Christ. Then all that was made in that exchange is null and void, as if it never happened. This is why we fight hard to keep our salvation, for it's only through repentance that we can recover that exchange that Christ made for us.

It is like a woman who just divorced a man, or a man who just divorced a woman, who is in misery, and when they meet in the store the woman or the man goes back into a relationship with that person that they just divorced. Thus, the spirit comes back seven times stronger, along with other evil spirits.

The next part of the definition of *climb* states: "to get into or out of clothing with some haste or effort," so the clothing we wear is an indicator of our walk or climb with Christ. In the world, clothing can tell a person whether they have high self-esteem, or if they are an easy person to persuade to have sex, or if the person is smart, or rich, or dumb, or poor.

Now, if these are all the things that the world knows about, how much more does the spiritual realm know about you by the way you dress. Now, don't be ridiculous by wearing clothes that are overkill when you should dress casually, and don't dress down when you have to dress up.

The Word of God states how you should dress; the garments you wear are the indicators of your walk with God and the glory of the God that you walk with. Why do you think that Paul was able to send a piece of his clothing to someone who was sick when he could not be there? It was because God led him to get the piece of clothing that not only made him look good, but that was set apart and was already anointed by God for the purpose of healing. Never mind that the clothes you wear physically represent the clothes you wear spiritually on your spirit man.

When you dress respectably, then your spirit man is dressed respectably, thus when you cast out the devil, your spirit is claiming the ground. Why should a demon respect a person's spirit when their spirit has no respect for themselves? Here is another aspect of your personal walk with God. You were in the world and you now come to God, or you are a person who has backslidden. It now takes an effort to get out of the clothes that you put on when the world clothed you.

Yeah, that's right, when you wore all those miniskirts and tight t-shirts—and for the men, baggy pants that look like they were around when Jesus was physically on the earth and those chains—what do you think those are? You think that it is just for style, but that's a representation of what your spirit has wrapped all over you.

For those of you who stay in the presence of God, He wraps a cloak around you. He robes you in kingly and queenly garments that are softer than silk and gentler than linen. But for those people who are newly saved, He now must help you get out of those clothes that you wore when you were wrapped in sin. God has to help you change the way you dress, because the clothes of the world are actually used as a prison to hold you in, in case you were to ever realize that they were to keep you from growing in God and to keep you from casting out the devil.

So now, it takes some effort from you and work from God to transform you into the king and queen that you were meant to originally be. And all of this work has to be done fast, because God is a person who is always climbing up the mountain.

If you think that's crazy, read:

Judges 6:34 Evangelical Heritage Version (EHV)
"The Spirit of the Lord clothed Gideon. He blew the ram's horn, and the clan of Abiezer was called out to follow him."

Acts 19:12 Evangelical Heritage Version (EHV)
"So that even handkerchiefs or aprons that had touched his skin were carried away to the sick; their illnesses left them, and the evil spirits went out of them."

One of the transitive senses says "to go upward on or along, to the top of, or over." When we climb, we climb to the top of the thing that holds us back. We push past all the opposition that holds us back from going into the next area, where God can grant us the favor and the rewards for the labor that we do with Him by climbing up that mountain. The other word says "to grow up or over."

As we continue to walk in Christ and continue to grow in Him, we can become giants for Christ. For too long, the giants have only been considered the enemy of God, and God doesn't have any giants. Well, it's time to tell you that God has some giants.

There are righteous giants in the land, but they are asleep—it's time to wake them up.

I say this because "to grow up or over" means that the thing that you are facing is smaller than the person fighting it, which is you. When you stand over something, you are looking down on that object. Now I know what it is to look down on things, and the thing may look mean and heavy—but in fact you're able to pick up that thing, and you can either squash it, or you can throw it so far that it turns into a ball of gas. It also means, when you stand over something, that that thing is already defeated and you are the victor; that's why, when you walk knowing this information, you have conquered all the ground you walk on. That also means that when the devil takes a captive, he hangs them upside down on their head so they don't walk on their feet, and they lose all feeling and the ability to walk, lest they realize that they can overcome in that arena. When you grow up and over, you defeat that demonic spirit in the name of the Lord Jesus Christ. Well now, what does it mean to *defeat* the devil?

Defeat (transitive verb) From Latin: to do

1) Obsolete: destroy

2) a) nullify; b) frustrate

3) to win victory over: beat

This war was already over the moment that Jesus said, "It is finished." The war for eternity is over; the

Lord Jesus defeated the devil. He utterly destroyed the devil—He made all of the weapons of the devil null and void, so therefore there is no more power in the weapons of the devil over my life and the lives of them that believe in the Lord Jesus Christ. He made sure that all of the things that the devil has are outdated and are all old and of no use in the attack on our souls. And you know why? Because when Jesus defeated the devil, Jesus went to win the victory over the devil, over sin, and over every minion in hell. You see that Jesus beat and has beaten all of hell. He went so far as to even frustrate the plans of the devil for your souls. He went and nullified every contract that was put out to make an assassination attempt against your soul, and the thing that makes all of this worth our while is that the same Jesus that did that is the same Jesus that lives in us. So now, what is it that is stopping you from working in Christ?

Now, I took the liberty to look up the word *frustrate.*

Frustrate:

1) a) to balk or defeat in an endeavor; b) to induce feelings of discouragement in

2) a) to make ineffectual: bring to nothing; b) impede, obstruct; c) to make invalid or of no effect

So, when Jesus said those three words, He frustrated the plans of the demonic realm. He defeated their endeavor to hold the world hostage. He gave them a feeling of discouragement in their attempts to overrun us, to destroy us; their plans have come to nothing. The Lord Jesus cut off the road of their success. He has shut them apart from their source of power, that power to choose—the choice to choose Jesus as Lord and Savior, or not. All of the things that the devil has have turned ineffectual in the attack against us. Nothing they do can take our life in the Lord Jesus; their contract that was made at the fall of man has just expired and turned invalid, and therefore all previously planned attacks and raids are of no effect. The works of the devil have become nullified.

Nullified:

1) make null; specially to make legally null and void

2) to make of no value or consequence

When God defeated the devil, He went and nullified his workings that he was planning to unleash on the world. Jesus even went and did all this by the law, so that there will be no exception to it. All of the things that the devil throws at us, we decide whether they are acceptable or not; everything that is of value to the enemy has turned to nothing. The currency down there has dropped to nothingness, and there are no more consequences for all that we have done in that past. They have been paid for by the God of heaven and earth. The only thing that we decide now is whether we repent or not from our sins, but other than that we have been set free to move in the things of God. For we are a part of God, for those of us that do believe in the Lord God Almighty, and it is for the Lord God alone that we have been made more than conquerors. So now, my brethren, let us move into the destiny that Christ has ordained for us to walk in as more than conquerors.

As you walk as a conqueror in Jesus Christ, you now overcome the enemy. Now the way the word *overcome* is used here is like this: "Overcome suggests getting the better of, with difficulty or after hard struggle." So, sometimes after you have a hard battle and you think that you won't be able to make it, you miraculously make it through, overcoming the obstacle that held you back from getting your blessing for so long.

The power of God is upon me now to declare the working power of the Lord. You overthrow the devil from his seat of power when you face hard opposition, and you keep your face in God, and you push through all persecution, overthrowing the reign of evil over your life.

You are now free to serve the Lord.

Psalm 116:16 Evangelical Heritage Version (EHV)

> *"Ah, Lord, truly I am your servant.*
> *I am your servant, the son of your maidservant.*
> *You opened my chains."*

I have overcome the world because the Lord has overcome the world, so therefore I can rest in the

Lord, for I can now take back the land that is rightfully mine. For the Spirit of the Lord is upon me to declare freedom to the captives, richness to the poor, healing to the sick, and restoration to the robbed.

Now, the last part of *conqueror* is "overthrow," which stresses the bringing down or destruction of existing power; ex.: violently overthrow the old regime.

Now, I didn't come up with the definition; that is the definition that is in Webster's dictionary. The way a conqueror moves is by overthrowing the old regime to put in place a new one.

What is the new regime? The new regime is the one that the conqueror brings into the land, and it is he or she that declares the laws and bylaws that the inhabitants of the land must yield themselves to.

Conquerors are those who seek God's face, those who walk their territory, those who go and seek out where the breech in the wall is. Because where there is a hole in the wall, most assuredly there is a kingdom that is starting a rebellion against the current reigning kingdom that is on the throne.

And it is those who are foolish that say, "There is no demonic spirit that is against me. I am more than fine; there is no enemy after my soul." That is where you can easily know that that person is conquered by that thing, whatever it may be.

The rebellion against that demonic force is coming

to take down the current reign of oppression over your life, but the thing about this is that it is a two-way thing. You see, for those of you who are just saved and for those of you who have been saved for many years—there is a difference. Those who just got saved—in order for you to gain the land that you originally lost, it is an even bigger battle, for you have to reset the boundaries back to the way your life should have been before you went and messed around with the devil. I mean, after you have accepted Jesus as Lord and Savior, the battle gets even more intense because it is you that is leading a rebellion against the current, reigning king—in this case, that devil that you let run your life for so many years. You see, if God is not on the throne of your land, then that means that the devil can easily over-throw you, because you hold no power in yourself. It is God alone who can beat the devil; you see, when you gave yourself to the devil and didn't choose God, it allowed the enemy to reign.

You have to choose a king to serve—if it is not God, then it is the devil who will take the land. Now you just got saved, so you have to go back into the land that kicked you out.

You see, if you were to stay in the land and realize who God is, then the devil would have to leave immediately. So that unclean spirit exiles you out of the land and you are thrown into a dry land, far enough so that you won't know where you are, but close enough to where you are in his power. So, you must yield to his power and his laws and bylaws, only because you gave that unclean spirit authority over your life. Now you have the light, and your light brought down the wall—that very wall that kept you bound to serve that demonic, oppressive spirit—and you can't run from the boundary that it set. That wall fell around you the minute that you said, "God, save me!"

You walk up to the city wall and you let out such a shout that it will bring down the wall of that oppressive spirit, and little by little, bit by bit, you lead a rebellion against the reigning kingdom of darkness over your land. As time goes by, you enter into the palace and say, "Get off my throne, for I come in the name of the King of Glory! I have been authorized to kill you, devil, so get off my land!" Then that devil will try to remind you of your past life, but Jesus said, "Let the redeemed of the Lord say so!" Then you say, "I have been redeemed by the blood of the Lamb!" And after the heated battle that will come from this, you have just taken back the land. You can now live freely and invite God to sit on the throne of your land, because you have come into the land with a king already over you. And from here, you can now reset the borders of your land and expand it. For you go out with the authority of the Lord, and you take the full borders of your inheritance—being your life—for Jesus, the Lord God, to rule over.

The moment you accept Christ, the power that once ruled your land with an iron fist has fallen. The moment that Christ said, "It is finished," all the land that was once held by that demonic spirit now has to be returned, and the devil must flee.

James 4:7 Evangelical Heritage Version (EHV)
"So, submit yourselves to God. Resist the Devil, and he will flee from you."

The power of God now takes hold of the inheritance of your land and gives it back to you as a spiritual inheritance. Not all at once, lest you get swallowed up by the land, but little by little so that you can keep what God has given to you, for it is also written:

Proverbs 10:22 Evangelical Heritage Version (EHV)
"The blessing of the Lord makes a person wealthy, and
       he adds no sorrow to it."

The power of the Lord is upon me to proclaim liberty to the captives and set free the heavy-laden.

Luke Soto

For We Are More Than Conquerors
How and why We are More Than a Conqueror

Romans 7:23 New Life Version (NLV)
"But there is a different law at work deep inside of me that fights with my mind. This law of sin holds me in its power because sin is still in me."

There, then, are two laws that I live by: the law of sin, and the law of righteousness. They are both the same law, but the law has been split both ways. In one way, it gratifies the flesh; in the other, it glorifies the Lord. In verse 22 he says that he delights in the law of the Lord and that it fills the inward man. But the inward man is the spirit man.

But I see another law in my members that wars against the law of my mind, and it then takes hold of me and brings me under the power of sin, which is in my members. Members are the body.

There is a war between the mind and the body taking place, in one situation that started the problem. Because he had fallen under the jurisdiction of sin, he must give in.

Thus, verse 24: *"There is no happiness in me! Who can set me free from my sinful old self?"*

And verse 25 says: *"God's Law has power over my mind, but sin still has power over my sinful old self. I thank God I can be free through Jesus Christ our Lord!"*

This, then, brings up what he says later, in Romans 12:2.

Romans 12:2 New King James Version (NKJV)
 "And do not be conformed to this world, but be transformed by the renewing of your mind, that you may prove what is that good and acceptable and perfect will of God."

Ephesians 6:13b New Life Version (NLV)

"…Then you will be able to stand in that sinful day. When it is all over, you will still be standing."

Ephesians 3:20 Worldwide English (New Testament) (WE) *"God can do much more than we ask him to do, or we even think of. He does it by his power which is working in us."*

Romans 7:7-8 The Voice (VOICE)
"So what is the story? Is the law itself sin? Absolutely not! It is the exact opposite. I would never have known what sin is if it were not for the law. For example, I would not have known that desiring something that belongs to my neighbor is sin if the law had not said, "You are not to covet." Sin took advantage of the commandment to create a constant stream of greed and desire within me; I began to want everything. You see, apart from the law, sin lies dormant."

The law was made to keep us in the good, but the way it turned out was different. For the only way to stay away from something is to first identify what it is, so you must first experience it. Sin took this occasion to come alive by using the law. Then Paul gives an example: he did not know covetousness but by the law, so for him to uphold the law he had to identify it, and it was not a bad thing. The law was made for this reason: to keep you from sinning. But sin took this opportunity, and he came alive by the words of the law (which shows you the power of God—He is the Law, so all things got to live) and by the words of the law he produced all manner of evil, so that man may fall into lawlessness and be consumed by the fires of hell.

For apart from the law sin was dead, but now that there was a right way to live, sin could pull men into the wrong way to live and destroy their palaces and take their authority and rule over them. People always want the ways of pleasure, so taking their land would be easy, and then sin would be able to establish his kingdom.

Now, because there was no law for the people to abide by, there was no sin—because what the people did was okay; they were innocent and did not know. But when Christ gave the law to the people, their sin was now able come alive and move among the people and use the opportunity to live life by killing their life. Now, how can sin revive and you die? The only way that that is possible is if sin was already dead once before, and you had life living in you.

There must have been some shaking in the atmosphere, like when Christ was on that cross and He rose again. But it was before that glorious resurrection. Somewhere before the time when Moses was around, and when Moses was there with the commandments, sin resurrected and ate out the souls of the people and took full reign and authority over them. So when sin revived, you died. And the very thing that was there to bring life into the land was found only to bring death—you only found it to produce death.

You obeyed the law, and you only produced death. Like Paul said earlier, we were only able to produce death, and when we were able to marry another man, we were now able to produce life.

Romans 7:11-12 New Life Version (NLV)
"Sin found a way to trap me by working through the Law. Then sin killed me by using the Law. The Law is holy. Each one of the Laws is holy and right and good."

Then sin had the right to kill me, because when the commandment of the law had come, sin had revived to kill me. For it had been put to sleep until the commandments came to life, and it was given to the people at that point. Then sin had a chance to enter the camp and kill us who had not abided in the law, for we were once lawless people. Like a leech, sin came and sucked the life out of the people, only leaving us with death. Then that means that the only thing we then had in us to produce was death.

We produce what we have inside of us, and the only thing that we had left was death, which was given to us from the time the commandments came from God. So, sin jumped on to the people and sucked the life out of us, taking from us all the richness of the land and taking the prosperity out of our lives. So the only thing that we had left was the law, and every time we obeyed the law we produced death, for we had no other choice. And when we did wrong, we were given over to death and sin; and when we did right, we produced sin and death and didn't fulfill the law. So we were damned if we did and damned if we didn't.

This doesn't mean that the law is bad. For God cannot have his people living in chaos and disorder, so for now He allowed it to enter the camp, to later come in and destroy that thing that held us bound to sin. Thus, Jesus said, "I didn't come to break the law, but I came to fulfill it."

Matthew 5:17 New Life Version (NLV)
"Do not think that I have come to do away with the Law of Moses or the writings of the early preachers. I have not come to do away with them but to complete them."

For when the law is finally fulfilled, then we are made free from the law of the husband that we were once married to. So that way, we may marry another and enter under His law. What this means is that the law that was meant to produce life was a guise that sin used to deceive us, and then it had the legal right to kill us by the very thing that had deceived us.

Then this means that the law is good and just and holy, for not just anyone can live by it and not just anyone can walk into it. For only those who are holy and just and good can uphold the law, without violation of its laws and codes and bylaws. So, for us, because of our lawless nature and chaotic behavior we were unable to hold onto the law, and by it were condemned to death. So therefore, the only one who can fulfill it would have to be the Holy One Himself, so He set them free from the chains of bondage. So, the law we live by is not of death but of life, which we have not yet acquired in this life.

The only way to begin this walk of life is by accepting the One who set us free from our previous captor. Yes, that's right—for now, Jesus is our captor. For when He took the keys from the domain of hell, Jesus Christ chose who was bound to Him and freed from the law of sin and death. For now death has no hold on Him; that's why the cross couldn't hold Him, the tomb couldn't retain Him, and hell couldn't burn Him. For He is the Risen Warrior, Christ—His name is God Almighty. He is God all by Himself! Do you know Him? For the chains of sin and death, they had to fall off by the blood of the Lamb that was sprinkled on the mercy seat and which was also poured out on the chains—which broke off at the sound of His thunderous voice saying, **"It is finished!"**

For We Are More Than Conquerors

Romans 7:13 New Life Version (NLV)
"Then does it mean that the Law, which is good, brought death to me? No, not at all! It was sin that did it. Sin brought death to me by the Law that is good. In that way, sin was shown to be what it is. So, because of the Law, sin becomes much more sinful."

That sin might max out in all that he did, he went as far as to produce sin through us; so that he might appear bigger than he did, he used us to reach the pinnacle of sin. In other words, sin was using the good in order to produce the bad, and the only ones who can do that are us humans. So, what is good to us has not really become death, but was turned around to be used as a tool for death. Sin, in other words, used the law as a tool to become exceedingly sinful, for the law was birthed at the beginning of time. And when God called it forth, sin revived, using the law as a tool to sap our strength and beauty and leaving us only with death—which we are now only producing. And the death that we bring is used by sin to become the exceedingly evil stronghold in our lives.

 The thing which is good is not bad at all; it was used as a tool for sin to create, and the reason he choose us is because he already died—something that is dead can't give life to something else, because it would dwindle away fast. But we have life in us, so that makes us a valuable object, because whatever we bring forth lasts for a long time—for God gave us His breath of life.

What is good has not become death to me, but sin—although it might appear as though sin was producing death in me through what is good, so that sin through the commandment might become exceedingly sinful.

Well, what is good? The only thing that Paul was saying here is the law. The law has not become death to me, but sin, though it might appear that sin was producing death in me. And we don't even know it, so through the commandment, sin might become exceedingly deadly. The laws that were given to us were spiritual laws to live by, but because I am carnal, I was sold under sin—because he had a legal right to sell me, for I was married into his law. Every time I did right, I made sin richer, and I died even further into darkness. And every time I did wrong, I was put under judgment, and then was able to be sold as a slave, making sin my taskmaster and ruler over my land.

Now here is Paul saying, "I am confused about what I am doing, because what I will to do, I don't practice it, but what I hate to do, that I carry out. Now, if I do what I hate to do, then I am fulfilling the law that is good because it came from God. But now the person that you see carrying out the wrong thing is not me, but sin that is doing it through me, for he has a legal right to do so." The only reason why he can come and do so is because of my flesh which is in me, and nothing good remains left in that part of me. And even though my will is present, I can't find it anywhere.

The reason we are moving into an area where we are no longer in control is because sin has obtained a legal right to sell us to the highest bidder in our lives. Thus, the strongholds come forth, and addictions break through, and then the generational curses begin.

Romans 7:1-3 The Voice (VOICE)
"My brothers and sisters who are well versed in the law, don't you realize that a person is subject to the law only as long as he is alive? So, for example, a wife is obligated by the law to her husband until his death; if the husband dies, she is freed from the parts of the law that relate to her marriage. If she is sleeping with another man while her husband is alive, she is rightly labeled an adulteress. But if her husband dies, she is free from the law and can marry another man. In such a case, she is not an adulteress."

Do you know that it is by the law that we live by that we have been saved by the blood of the Lamb? It is by the eternal power of God Almighty, who has saved us from the powers of sin and death; it is by His power alone that we have been saved. It was too high a price that no mortal man could pay, so the Eternal One, the Almighty God alone, had the value and then some to give to the people of sin and death. But because it was not theirs, He used it to pay off our debt, and then He called it back to Himself.

For no man can take away the value of the man who

had to fight for it. It was the law of God that was given to us. We think that we killed God by our own sin, but if He had not come, we would all burn in hell. So, who are we to say that we killed God and that we are responsible for His death? Do you not know that He lives, and He cannot die?

Isaiah 55:11 The Voice (VOICE)
  "So, it is when I declare something.
  My word will go out and not return to Me empty,
  But it will do what I wanted;
  it will accomplish what I determined."

So, long before us, God said that He would die for our sins so that we might have life once again and know this man who was our Creator. In the garden of Gethsemane, the name of the mountain that he was on the night that he was brought before the Sanhedrin means *"pressing of the olive."* But in this sense of *pressing,* the olive was mashed into pulp, and then for the final oil, the stone had to press down on the pulp of the olive so that they could get all of the oil from that olive. We call Jesus the "Anointed One"; in order for the anointing to come forth, Jesus had to be beaten to take His oil, and then He would have to be pulp and have a stone rolled onto Him to take the rest of His oil. And when they took away His stone, He sent an angel with a memo saying, "I am not here, but risen; I will see you in Galilee."

 You see, it was not by our lawlessness that we killed Christ; we did what we were told to do. He did it to fulfill the law that was sent before us to be carried out. You see, it was not religiousness that killed Him, it was the mercy of God that came to free us from the marital law of sin. That is what Christ came for. For don't you know, brethren, that the law has dominion over a man if he lives? That means that we, as humans, must abide by the law throughout the entirety of our lives. And if we are married to sin, we have to abide by the law of sin throughout the entirety of his life.

Now, here is something interesting: if we are the bride of Christ and we are bound to sin, that means we are married to sin—and then if Christ came and we married Him while married to sin, we would be called an adulteress. The only way to get rid of a name like that would be if sin dies. Christ would have to kill sin for Him to marry us, and that would not only allow us a new life, but also free us from the law that kept us bound to sin.

Romans 6:19-23 Holman Standard Christian Bible (HSCB) "I am using a human analogy because of the weakness of your flesh. For just as you offered the parts of yourselves as slaves to moral impurity, and to greater and greater lawlessness, so now offer them as slaves to righteousness, which results in sanctification. For when you were slaves of sin, you were free from allegiance to righteousness. So what fruit was produced then from the things you are now ashamed of? For the end of those things is death. But now, since you have been liberated from sin and have become enslaved to God, you have your fruit, which results in sanctification—and the end is eternal life! For the wages of sin is death, but the gift of God is eternal life in Christ Jesus our Lord."

Paul had to hold back when he was speaking to the people reading this letter, because their flesh would not be able to hold the power that was about to come upon them. So, the same way that you were slaves of uncleanliness and everything you did was unclean, in the same way you are to act now as slaves to righteousness, so that everything you do can be holy before a Holy God. Well, why is that? Because when you were bound to sin, righteousness had no reason to be there—because it's holy and you're not, so it would turn away. Before you got saved, what fruit did you produce that you had to show? It was nothing, because later all your production would be taken away or be burned up. That road was death—that is what you were on, and death doesn't produce... anything at all. And now that you have switched to God, whatever you produce you have a reason to produce it, and it is made to holiness. And when it comes time for the end of that thing, we go into everlasting life.

"For the wages of sin is death, but the gift of God is eternal life." So, after working in sin, your day's wages would be death, nothing, a waste. But the wages of God now give us more. We are now given eternal life after we are finished working the field with God. And the wages He gives are a gift. Because we now live it in Jesus Christ our Lord.

Now, Jesus just entered Jerusalem, and the title in most Bibles would say: "The triumphal entry into Jerusalem."

Jesus had for the first time stepped into Jerusalem, and they threw Him a conqueror's feast. How can this be, if He had not yet been crucified and risen again? Because He had already stepped into the field as more than a conqueror. The only way to treat Him was by throwing him a feast.

Because in the beginning of time, before the world was made, He threw down—He took down the devil and his angels. So He had already won, and now that He had entered Jerusalem all creation knew it by the sense that they felt—that freedom was coming. All hell broke loose when He came from the Mount of Olives, an area where the country got their oil from. And He had come for the first time, and yet was received as a hero that had come back from war. And He was already triumphant, because the cross couldn't hold Him, the grave couldn't keep Him, and hell couldn't bind Him. And now, all of creation was set free from the grasp of sin. For in the earlier chapter, it was said that He taught with great authority, so why stop there when you can walk in it, too? When the donkey stepped through the city gate, the authority of God took over the whole city.

Now, the first act that was done in Jerusalem was that Jesus cleansed the temple and got rid of the defilement that had been brought in and allowed to stay there. And it offended all the religious priests in the whole city, because it showed that they were not doing their job. And now they had to explain why the mess was there.

Romans 6:1-7 The Voice (VOICE)
"How should we respond to all of this? Is it good to persist in a life of sin so that grace may multiply even more? Absolutely not! How can we die to a life where sin ruled over us and then invite sin back into our lives? Did someone forget to tell you that when we were initiated into Jesus the Anointed through baptism's ceremonial washing, we entered into His death? Therefore, we were buried with Him through this baptism into death so that just as God the Father, in all His glory, resurrected the Anointed One, we, too, might walk confidently out of the grave into a new life. To put it another way: if we have been united with Him to share in a death like His, don't you understand that we will also share in His resurrection? We know this: whatever we used to be with our old sinful ways has been nailed to His cross. So, our entire record of sin has been canceled, and we no longer have to bow down to sin's power. A dead man, you see, cannot be bound by sin."

Should we stay in sin so that grace may stay in abundance? Certainly not, because we died to sin. If we are dead, how can we come back to life again? We can't, so that area of sin has been cut out of us and the door has been shut to it. We who were baptized into God were really baptized into the death He died for us on the cross. Therefore, now we may be buried with Him; so, the same way I was buried is the same way I get to resurrect with Him into the glory of the Father and get to have a new life. This is what Jesus meant when He said, "You must be born again." Once you are baptized, you die that death on the cross—and that also means that you are now buried with Jesus in order to be resurrected by the glory of the Father. You may experience a new life, now freed from sin.

This is the famous story of Romeo and Juliet. If you notice, the whole mishap was set up by the friar, a monk, a man of the church who knew the prince. And the bride had to fake her death, and when she woke up, she would marry. So here, Jesus sees us dead, and He dies for our ailment. And then—here's the twist—she wakes from her death sleep, and the dead prince awakens in all His glory from the Father, and the two get married.

God is willing to share the work, for the Bible says, *"If you share in my death, then I will also share with you my life."*

Romans 6:5 Holman Christian Standard Bible (HCSB)
"For if we have been joined with Him in the likeness of His death, we will certainly also be in the likeness of His resurrection."

In other words, if you pay the suffering now, then

you get your rewards later. And this is only possible because we went through it with Him. If you were united in His death, then you are united now that He has come alive.

We now know that our old self was crucified with Him. And how do we know that? You got baptized in the name of Jesus, and all that was so that you might crucify the flesh, and so that the old self of sin would be done away with, so sin is no longer your owner. Because what good is a dead slave that is not producing anything? So, they have to be cut off. For the way the slave system worked was, "You serve me till I die, or you are dead, and then I take the next person in your family." But the good news is that you died the moment you were baptized. You died to sin.

Romans 6:8-9 Holman Christian Standard Bible (HCSB) "Now if we died with Christ, we believe that we will also live with Him, because we know that Christ, having been raised from the dead, will not die again. Death no longer rules over Him."

Now, if we were there in His death, we believe that He will resurrect us, and we will live with Him. The day that Christ was resurrected, death had no hold on Him because He had already died a death, and He was still living. So now the life He is living He lives to God, and the death that He died He died to sin—once, for everyone.

Because of this, it is now possible that we can live

to God. Because death has no hold on us, for it is no longer I who live, but Christ lives in me. So now, the thing I have to do is to be done with sin and to not listen to its evils, because now I can produce life. So, don't let us use the body God gave us to sin, so that sin can build and use us as a tool of unrighteousness—but let's live the way we should and present ourselves as a righteous tool to God. For sin has no more control over us, for we are not under law, but under God.

Romans 8:1-2 Worldwide English (New Testament) *(WE) "So now those who belong to Christ Jesus will not be judged. The Spirit gives life in Christ Jesus. And the law of the Spirit has set me free from the law of wrong things, and the law of death."*

I have no condemnation on me, because I walk a Holy Spirit-led life and because I don't follow the law of sin and death. And I don't follow the law of sin and death because Christ has made me free.

That means that even though we sin, there is no condemnation on us because the way we live, we live it in the Spirit. It is the Spirit-led life that keeps me from indwelling sin. Because the law that I am under is different from the law of sin and death; the law of grace frees me from my flesh and allows me to move freely in my spirit man to do the things of God. And the only way to find this law is in Jesus Christ, because Christ was the one to carry the law, and not us. So now, the only way to be under that law is by going to the One who has the law already inside of Him, and then if we connect to the source, we get covered by the law that is in that person's spirit.

Romans 8:3-4 The Message (MSG)
"God went for the jugular when he sent his own Son. He didn't deal with the problem as something remote and unimportant. In his Son, Jesus, he personally took on the human condition, entered the disordered mess of struggling humanity in order to set it right once and for all. The law code, weakened as it always was by fractured human nature, could never have done that. The law always ended up being used as a Band-Aid on sin instead of a deep healing of it. And now what the law code asked for but we couldn't deliver is accomplished as we, instead of redoubling our own efforts, simply embrace what the Spirit is doing in us."

For what the law couldn't do in that it was weak through the flesh, God did in sending His Son in the form of sinful flesh on account of sin; He condemned sin.

So, the thing that made the perfect law was that it was carried by the flesh, which left the law unfulfilled. Because you have to be led in the Spirit to carry it out, and now what the law could not do, God did by sending His Son in the likeness of sinful flesh. He was undercover, really; He was always perfect, but the cover was that He was just a man.

The account of sin was His cause, and the fulfillment of this allowed Him to condemn sin.

The law that was given to us was so heavy, and the flesh is so weak that it could not uphold the weight of that law. For example, if a person who can only lift 20 lbs. of weight were to bench press 300 lbs., they would be crushed and die. And then whoever can take the weight off of this struggling body, that is the person we subject ourselves to. And the part of our body that was used to lift the weight is now damaged to the point where we cannot use it anymore, and somewhere back in time whatever was of no use was cut off. And God says in His laws that the priests cannot be maimed. If they are, then they cannot go into the temple of God. And now, "What the law couldn't do in that it was weak through the flesh"; the law that you hold is only as strong as the person who carries it. So then a law that is heavy and strong that is passed on to a weak and lawless flesh, that law then crushes the body, and it is made weak because the person connected to the law is weak. So now that the law was weak, the only person who would be able to help was God Himself, and so He sent His Son in the form of a sinful man, but it was only a disguise. Because sin didn't know that Christ had come yet, and when it came down to the sin area, He condemned it to hell. And sin was like, "How can this man do this stuff?"

That is why, after the Holy Spirit descended on Jesus, that He was tempted by the devil, because the devil said, "There is a man who has some power in His Spirit, and He is a lot different than all the other people God has sent before." He said, "If you are really the Son of God," but to keep his cover Jesus said that you shall worship God alone, and the devil flew away from Him. He was waiting for another chance to attack Jesus. Now Jesus was more than a conqueror already, so that means that the devil had to ask God to tempt him, and God must have said, "Yes, but to this point only." And like Job, Jesus stood strong.

Romans 8:4 Holman Christian Standard Bible (HCSB)

"In order that the law's requirement would be accomplished in us who do not walk according to the flesh but according to the Spirit."

That means that there was a daily requirement of righteous living for the flesh to fulfill. But because I had died from the law coming to this lawless body, my flesh was given over to sin, and I was unable to fulfill the law of God, and I was bound so my spirit man couldn't move. But the moment Christ died and rose again I was unbound in my spirit man and could live under a new rule. Those laws are by grace and mercy, and the righteous requirement for the flesh has been paid for by the Lord Jesus Christ who, in becoming a man, freed all people from the requirement of righteousness. But the freedom that is given and the fulfillment of the law is only given to those who walk according to the Spirit, and the only way that is possible is if you believe in God Almighty.

Romans 8:5 Holman Christian Standard Bible (HCSB)
"For those who live according to the flesh think about the things of the flesh, but those who live according to the Spirit, about the things of the Spirit."

For those living according to the flesh set their minds on the things of the flesh. But those who live according to the Spirit think about the things of the Spirit.

The reason why is because of what is said in Romans 6:16-17.

Romans 6:16-17 New Century Version (NCV)
"Surely you know that when you give yourselves like slaves to obey someone, then you are really slaves of that person. The person you obey is your master. You can follow sin, which brings spiritual death, or you can obey God, which makes you right with him. In the past you were slaves to sin—sin controlled you. But thank God, you fully obeyed the things that you were taught."

It says, "That whom you present yourselves slaves to obey you are slaves to that one whom you obey." For you live according to the flesh, and you then set your mind on the things of the flesh. But the reason why we have what we have is because we are slaves of the Holy Spirit, and then we set our minds on the things of the Spirit. For like God said, as a man thinks, so is he.

Romans 8:5-8 The Message (MSG)
"Those who think they can do it on their own end up obsessed with measuring their own moral muscle but never get around to exercising it in real life. Those who trust God's action in them find that God's Spirit is in them—living and breathing God! Obsession with self in these matters is a dead end; attention to God leads us out into the open, into a spacious, free life. Focusing on the self is the opposite of focusing on God. Anyone completely absorbed in self ignores God, ends up thinking more about self than God. That person ignores who God is and what he is doing. And God isn't pleased at being ignored."

For to be carnally-minded is death, but to be spiritually-minded is life and peace. For the way that you live your life is the way that you reap the works of the field.

You live in sin and sin produces death in you, and at the end of the day you have nothing but a wasteful life—unproductive, and your day's wages is death. And you produce death, because you think carnally while you work the field. You obeyed death and became his slave and then set your mind on carnal thinking, and as a man thinketh so is he; because you set your mind on the things of the flesh, and flesh only works now for death.

For those of us that believe and live in the Spirit work the field and produce a great harvest that God will enjoy, and at the end of the day our wages are eternal life, because we walk in a law that allows us to produce life. Because as we worked, we obeyed God and became His slaves, and we were spiritually-minded, and He added all the blessing that He said He would unto us.

So, the equation for death is: sin + flesh + disobedience = death, waste, unproductiveness, and slavery

 And the equation for life is: obedience + grace + Spirit living = eternal life, productiveness, lifelong blessing, and freedom

Isaiah 9:6 Evangelical Heritage Version (EHV)
"For to us a child is born.
To us a son is given.
The authority to rule will rest on his shoulders.
He will be named:
    Wonderful Counselor,
    Mighty God,
    Everlasting Father,
    Prince of Peace."

In modern days the government is also known as the law, so knowing that, the law rests on His shoulders, and He shall be called wonderful Counselor, mighty God, everlasting Father, Prince of peace.

His name is Counselor, just like a law interpreter. So now you are saying, "God, I ran into a problem, and I don't know what to do. Can you counsel me on this problem?" Because when He walks, He walks with law and order in His steps, and it's not just any law—it's the fulfilled law that He walks with.

So now, if we walk in His steps and ask, "What would Jesus do?" we now walk also in law and order in such a way that we can live by the law. For He fulfilled the law and is living in us, and the closer we walk, God says "he no longer lives but I in him," for "I was crucified at the cross with Him." Any problems with the law, God will take care of it and now makes us whole in His new law.

If you read the previous chapters, you know that it is faith in God that circumcises the heart of a man who believes in Him, and that if we were judged it would be by the law against sin, but sin is what acknowledges the law. Christ came, and through His blood He passed over all the sin that was present (so it was kind of like a clean slate), and now because of that there is no more boasting, because it is not in the new law. The old law allowed that, but the law of faith is separate from the old law. And God can judge us all, because He is not only the God of the Jews, but also the God of the Gentiles. Because now, whoever believes in him is circumcised though faith, and He may judge them as well as the circumcised by faith.

Romans 4:1-4 New Century Version (NCV)
"So what can we say that Abraham, the father of our people, learned about faith? If Abraham was made right by the things he did, he had a reason to brag.

But this is not God's view, because the Scripture says, "Abraham believed God, and God accepted Abraham's faith, and that faith made him right with God." When people work, their pay is not given as a gift, but as something earned."

What can you say about Abraham now? If Abraham was judged by works, he would have something to boast about, but not before God. Because the scriptures say, that "Abraham believed God, and it was accounted unto him as righteousness." And now to him who works it is not grace, but debt. "Works" being all the things that were done in the past, like sacrifices, and all of that. If that were to be done again it would be not done out of grace, but out of lack, for debt is lack.

Romans 4:5 New Life Version (NLV)
"If a man has not worked to be saved, but has put his trust in God Who saves men from the punishment of their sins, that man is made right with God because of his trust in God."

The person who does not do the works anymore but believes in the One who paid for us already, it's his faith that is accounted to him as righteousness, and he gives an example. David says, "Blessed is the man to whom God imputes righteousness apart from works; blessed are those whose lawless deeds are forgiven him and whose sins are covered; blessed is the man to whom the Lord shall not impute sin."

Romans 4:6-12 The Message (MSG)

*"David confirms this way of looking at it, saying
that the one who trusts God to do the putting-every-
thing-right without insisting on having a say in it is
one fortunate man:*

Fortunate those whose crimes are carted off,
  whose sins are wiped clean from the slate.
Fortunate the person against
  whom the Lord does not keep score.
*Do you think for a minute that this blessing is only
pronounced over those of us who keep our religious
ways and are circumcised? Or do you think it
possible that the blessing could be given to those
who never even heard of our ways, who were never
brought up in the disciplines of God? We all agree,
don't we, that it was by embracing what God did for
him that Abraham was declared fit before God?
 Now think: Was that declaration made before or
after he was marked by the covenant rite of circumcision? That's right, before he was marked. That
means that he underwent circumcision as evidence
and confirmation of what God had done long before
to bring him into this acceptable standing with
himself, an act of God he had embraced with his
whole life.*
*And it means further that Abraham is father of all
people who embrace what God does for them while
they are still on the "outs" with God, as yet uniden-
tified as God's, in an "uncircumcised" condition. It
is precisely these people in this condition who are*

*called "set right by God and with God"! Abraham is
also, of course, father of those who have undergone
the religious rite of circumcision not just because
of the ritual but because they were willing to live in
the risky faith-embrace of God's action for them, the
way Abraham lived long before he was marked by
circumcision."*

Now if Abraham's works did not justify him, but his
belief in God made him righteous, what then made
his belief in God righteous? Was it the circumcision?
No, because it was his faith before he was circumcised that made him righteous.

And the sign of circumcision was a seal of righteousness and his faith in God before he was circumcised.

And this happened so that he might be the father of
the uncircumcised, and so that he might show that
righteousness is imputed to those who believe in
God but are uncircumcised, as well as to those who
are circumcised and live by God.

Therefore, the righteousness of God is given to those
who believe and live by Him.

The way Abraham was walking with God, it was
so that he could be the father of those who are
circumcised and sealed in covenant with God. Also,
he would be the covering for the people who are
uncircumcised, by what God did when he counted
Abraham's belief as righteousness. This is saying

that well before Abraham got circumcised, God made him righteous, so we who are not circumcised can be counted by the same righteousness he had if we believe in God. And that opens the door of the blessing that Abraham received, because if he wanted to go to the next level, he had to do this one thing, and that was to be circumcised.

And the rest is history.

The definition of *impute*:

Impute:

1) to lay the responsibility or blame for (something) often falsely or unjustly

2) to credit or ascribe (something) to a person or a cause: attribute

Synonym: ascribe

Attribute:

1) an inherent characteristic; also, an accidental quality

2) an object closely associated with or belonging to a person, thing, or office, especially: such an object used for identification in painting or sculpture

3) a word ascribing a quality, especially: adjective

Synonym: quality_

Ascribe:

to refer to a supposed cause, source, or author

synonym: attribute, assign, impute, accredit

Ascribe means to lay something to the account of a person or thing. *Ascribe* suggests an inferring, conjecturing of cause, quality, authorship.

Romans 4:13-15 New Century Version (NCV)
"Abraham and his descendants received the promise that they would get the whole world. He did not receive that promise through the law, but through being right with God by his faith. If people could receive what God promised by following the law, then faith is worthless. And God's promise to Abraham is worthless, because the law can only bring God's anger. But if there is no law, there is nothing to disobey."

The promise that God made was that the world would be given to him; he was an heir. Being made an heir was, in fact, for all who believe in Him, and not just Abraham. For it was by the righteousness that is acquired by faith that this gift was bestowed to him.

That means that the law is a guideline then, because if those who live by the law are the heirs, then faith is made void and righteousness is of no value. And the promise is made to no effect, meaning that the whole thing that God spoke as a vow to Abraham was a fake, it was a lie—and God doesn't lie.

The law is what brings the wrath. Then those who

are of the law are really of wrath. And I don't think God would make a vow to give the world to the people of wrath. For where there is no law there is no transgression. *Transgression* means infringement or violation of a law, command, or duty.

For where there is no law there is no violation of a command; that is what Paul is saying.

Romans 4:16-20 New Living Translation (NLT)
"So the promise is received by faith. It is given as a free gift. And we are all certain to receive it, whether or not we live according to the law of Moses, if we have faith like Abraham's. For Abraham is the father of all who believe. That is what the Scriptures mean when God told him, "I have made you the father of many nations." This happened because Abraham believed in the God who brings the dead back to life and who creates new things out of nothing. Even when there was no reason for hope, Abraham kept hoping—believing that he would become the father of many nations. For God had said to him, "That's how many descendants you will have!" And Abraham's faith did not weaken, even though, at about 100 years of age, he figured his body was as good as dead—and so was Sarah's womb. Abraham never wavered in believing God's promise. In fact, his faith grew stronger, and in this he brought glory to God."

So, the promise that was given to Abraham was given and made under faith. So the keeping of that law can be maintained under grace, then. And it is like that so that the promise is surety for all of Abraham's kids and for those under the law and those who walk with the same faith as Abraham. So, if we are not physically under his law with God, then we are connected to Abraham through our faith in God, which avails our faith in Jesus Christ and then is counted as righteousness unto the Lord. Wherever the blessing of Abraham is located for us to accept, it is in our faith in God that we get the blessing that He has for us to receive.

And it is proven to us, because it is written that *"I have made you the father of many nations."* How did he get the promise? Where was Abraham? He was in the presence of the One who he believed: God.

Romans 4:18-25 New Living Translation (NLT)
"Even when there was no reason for hope, Abraham kept hoping—believing that he would become the father of many nations. For God had said to him, "That's how many descendants you will have!" And Abraham's faith did not weaken, even though, at about 100 years of age, he figured his body was as good as dead—and so was Sarah's womb. Abraham never wavered in believing God's promise. In fact, his faith grew stronger, and in this he brought glory to God. He was fully convinced that God is able to do whatever he promises. And because of Abraham's faith, God counted him as righteous. And when God counted him as righteous, it wasn't just for Abraham's benefit. It was recorded for our

benefit, too, assuring us that God will also count us as righteous if we believe in him, the one who raised Jesus our Lord from the dead. He was handed over to die because of our sins, and he was raised to life to make us right with God."

He was at a point in life where hope was lost, due to his age, of bearing a son. He was too old a man to believe anything then, except what was spoken as a promise by God, who speaks of those things which do not exist as though they did. Meaning that it had already happened. That is saying to those dead things that "you're old, but your kid is still going to be a father of many nations, and your blessing shall be on him as well." That is the way God must have spoken to Abraham when this blessing came about.

So, contrary to what hope had for him, he still believed. Well, what is hope?

Hope:

a desire accompanied by expectation or belief in fulfillment.

Contrary to his expectation, he believed in the fulfilled product already. So that is why he became the father of many nations.

And not being weak in faith, he considered his body already dead. He had to act, then, as a young man would act in order to carry out what he had received as a promise. He did not consider the deadness of Sarah's womb, or his deadness. He then had to walk with the promise through the area of unbelief, and instead of getting weaker as time went by, he got stronger in God, giving God the glory.

This, then, brings up the point that God is the One who made the promise, and he was convinced of what He had promised and that He was also able to perform the action.

And it was in that that his faith was accounted as righteousness, and it was not only for him that it is written it was imputed to him. It was for us to see that it can also happen for us. Abraham was not only the pioneer but also the example of righteous faith.

And now to us it will be imputed—to us who believe in the One who raised Jesus up from the dead, who was delivered up for our offenses and raised for our justification.

Romans 5:1-5 Evangelical Heritage Version (EHV) *"Therefore, since we have been justified by faith, we have peace with God through our Lord Jesus Christ. Through him we also have obtained access by faith into this grace in which we stand. And we rejoice confidently on the basis of our hope for the glory of God. Not only this, but we also rejoice confidently in our sufferings, because we know that suffering produces patient endurance, and patient endurance produces tested character, and tested character produces hope. And hope will not put us to shame, because God's love has been poured out into our hearts by the Holy Spirit, who was given to us."*

So, being justified by faith, the Jesus in whom we believe has made us to be at peace with God, so no longer am I in a situation with God where He is in one of two places: both in His anger and at war with us. And it was by faith in Jesus who has given Himself for us that He has justified us, where God is no longer angry or at war with us. And now we have the peace of God. And this same faith in God has given us access to God's grace, the very grace which we stand in and live on. That way we can't say that we can't forgive, then, because the grace that you thought you were in isn't really there, and you're really not shown any grace because you didn't show any grace. This faith also gives us access to rejoice in God's glory.

So, this glory has made us at peace with God and one with Him. It justifies us from the law and as heirs to the blessing of Abraham. It is the same faith in Jesus Christ that we have that measures us at the same level of faith that Abraham had. And the grace we are shown by God is same grace we can give to others, through this faith in Jesus Christ.

And on top of that, the time that we shine the most is in tribulation; that is where the glory of God that has been poured out on us comes forth. So, in other words, the storm you face brings out of you and draws forth the glory of God that is given to you. The power of God then shines forth every time you're in a battle. So, the time that I should actually thank God is when I am in the middle of a battle—

but then I remember, "*the battle is not mine, but the battle is the Lord's.*" I should praise God in the middle of this sickness—then I remember, "*Jesus is the great physician.*" When I have no food and bills are too high to pay—I remember, "*He is Jehovah Jireh, my provider.*" He is the one and only who is ever able to complete the work that He started through you. I am to give God praise and not worry, like He says in Matthew. So why should I worry about my life if God is the One who takes care of me, and in my trouble, He makes me to glory.

How I glory is through tribulation, which makes perseverance, and it's when I persevere that character is made in me. And when I have character, I have hope, and it is hope that makes faith what it is. When I believe God, hope is alive, and my belief is hope in God that He will do whatever things I need, knowing that He provides for all my needs. Because if I believe God, I am considered righteous, and I have not seen the righteous begging for bread.

Now this hope that we have does not disappoint, because the love that God has for us has been poured out into our hearts by the Holy Spirit who was given to us.

It was the hope of God that was and is poured out for us, and it fills our hearts. So now I can do all things through Christ who strengthens me, because it is the Holy Spirit who is in me that pours out this faith of God in my heart. I know that the hope I have in God will make me perfect as I continue this walk in Him. For He meets me, and it is He now who is in me, and it's His faith that makes me a Christian with the righteous faith. For it is the Holy Spirit that is in God that is also in me, and it is that faith that God has that has been poured out into my heart that fills me—and it allows Him the access to move in the way that only God can move.

Romans 5:6 Holman Christian Standard Bible (HCSB)
"For while we were still helpless, at the appointed moment, Christ died for the ungodly."

Here we have the Holy Spirit pouring out God's love on us, giving us hope during the time that we were not strong, so that we may endure the punishment of sin. *Punishment* meaning the heat, the fire, the beat down, until the time came for Jesus to come and get rid of this abuser who abuses the ungodly. So He gave us Gentiles a way out of the abuse, out of our problems: He died for the unrighteous so that they may become righteous. He came and showed us a love that changed the face of this world that was held hostage to sin and death. And here is the example:

Romans 5:7 Holman Christian Standard Bible (HCSB)
"For rarely will someone die for a just person— though for a good person perhaps someone might even dare to die."

For We Are More Than Conquerors

Romans 5:8-11 The Voice (VOICE)

"But think about this: while we were wasting our lives in sin, God revealed His powerful love to us in a tangible display—the Anointed One died for us. As a result, the blood of Jesus has made us right with God now, and certainly we will be rescued by Him from God's wrath in the future. If we were in the heat of combat with God when His Son reconciled us by laying down His life, then how much more will we be saved by Jesus' resurrection life? In fact, we stand now reconciled and at peace with God. That's why we celebrate in God through our Lord Jesus, the Anointed."

And now that the blood of the Lamb has been shed for us, if we accept Him it is us who have been saved from the wrath of God. The wrath that is stored up to be unleashed when He comes back— that is the wrath that we are saved from, for only those who believe in Jesus Christ are saved. And the man that does not know God is a sinner, and then he is considered an enemy of Him and he will face the wrath of God. But through the blood of Jesus he has been saved, and now—once enemies—we have the chance to become good friends. But in reality, you were made in heaven as a family member in Christ, and once living here, you got separated. And through Jesus, He has reconciled you to God, so you no longer are destroyed but are saved from the wrath through Jesus.

And now we can rejoice in God again—but in order

to rejoice, it is through Jesus that we rejoice, and in Him because He goes to the Father. So, through Jesus I can praise God and know that God can hear my praise, because He sits at the right hand of the Father, and He is always seated on the throne.

Through Jesus we have received the reconciliation, and it was only through Him, who was able to give us this gift.

Romans 5:12-14 The Voice (VOICE)
"Consider this: sin entered our world through one man, Adam; and through sin, death followed in hot pursuit. Death spread rapidly to infect all people on the earth as they engaged in sin. Before God gave the law, sin existed, but there was no way to account for it. Outside the law, how could anyone be charged and found guilty of sin? Still, death plagued all humanity from Adam to Moses, even those whose sin was of a different sort than Adam's. You see, in God's plan, Adam was a prototype of the One who comes to usher in a new day."

Therefore, through the sin of one man, sin entered; death entered through sin because the law that God gave Moses was not made yet. Sin then has no reason to live, so in reality all have died—because wherever sin is, death is also there. And since sin can't live, death came and reigned from Adam to Moses. How can He do that? The same way that we can praise God: through Jesus Christ. That is how He did it.

For We Are More Than Conquerors

Romans 5:15-17 The Message (MSG)

"Yet the rescuing gift is not exactly parallel to the death-dealing sin. If one man's sin put crowds of people at the dead-end abyss of separation from God, just think what God's gift poured through one man, Jesus Christ, will do! There's no comparison between that death-dealing sin and this generous, life-giving gift. The verdict on that one sin was the death sentence; the verdict on the many sins that followed was this wonderful life sentence. If death got the upper hand through one man's wrongdoing, can you imagine the breathtaking recovery life makes, sovereign life, in those who grasp with both hands this wildly extravagant life-gift, this grand setting-everything-right, that the one man Jesus Christ provides?"

So, this gift that is now given to us is not like the offense that was here, because we have the choice to accept the gift of God—unlike the offense, where we were born into it and have no choice; we have this offense because it is hereditary. But the same way that sin entered and ruled through one man's sin is the same way that God now entered and gave us the freedom to make the choice through One man named Jesus Christ, and His gift abounded to many.

Romans 5:12-14 (Part 2)

Death was the dominant power back then in the world; this is what happened from the first quarter of the beginning of time, from when Adam ate the fruit to the time that Moses gave the law. Sin entered, but it was to no real effect, but death used the sin that had entered the world and reigned in that time period. Even the righteous were under the rule of death. And when the law was given, sin revived and took over, because the law was there and in place. How can this be? Because like Paul said, "Sin cannot be imputed where there is no law." And those who were righteous and had not committed the acts that Adam did were still subject to death's rule.

Romans 5:18 Evangelical Heritage Version (EHV)
"So then, just as one trespass led to a verdict of condemnation for all people, so also one righteous verdict led to life-giving justification for all people."

The way the world was condemned was through the sin of one man. Now, that one man was made in the likeness of God. So how can the world be condemned, then? It was because it was given over to death the moment sin entered, because God brings conviction and not condemnation. The enemy is the one who brings this judgment through the reigning power of the ruler in that time, which would have to be death. How can death bring condemnation? Because sin was in the whole human race now, and death used sin as a gateway to enter the world, and then took over sin's place because sin only lives in the law. Death then can live where there is no law, but cannot live where there is law; but sin can live where there is law but cannot live without the law. So therefore, because that man who was placed as a prince to rule, who would go by the name of Adam, ate the fruit, in doing that he took himself off the reigning power and bowed down and gave his crown to death, who accepted the power then given to him by man. And it was legal, because there was no written law against it.

Later on, as time went by, the law was passed and sin then took over the place where death was reigning. And where death left off, sin picked up, because sin operates by the law, whereas death was outlawed and cast out of the seat of power, due to loopholes. And because man was already dead, sin came to power and used that seed, and that substance of life and the death that was given to man, and then turned it to worship himself, and in doing so we now have followed sin from the time of Moses till Jesus.

But now there was a Man who came down in the likeness of flesh, and He became a man but yet retained his power as God Almighty, and in fulfilling the scriptures, He fulfilled the law that was passed by death and passed by sin. And then He went and redeemed all who were righteous but yet slaves to sin, and slaves to death. And because hell was taking everything, He went down and took the keys from him and freed us all from the wrath that was for us. But He now can only free a person if they choose Him and believe in Him; otherwise, their ruler is still sin.

Courtroom hearing:

Job 36:2-33 New Living Translation (NLT)
"Let me go on, and I will show you the truth.
  For I have not finished defending God!

I will present profound arguments
  for the righteousness of my Creator.

I am telling you nothing but the truth,
  for I am a man of great knowledge.

God is mighty, but he does not despise anyone!
  He is mighty in both power and understanding.

He does not let the wicked live
  but gives justice to the afflicted.

He never takes his eyes off the innocent,
  but he sets them on thrones with kings
and exalts them forever.

If they are bound in chains
  and caught up in a web of trouble,

he shows them the reason.
  He shows them their sins of pride.

He gets their attention
  and commands that they turn from evil.

If they listen and obey God,
  they will be blessed with prosperity throughout
  their lives.
All their years will be pleasant.

For We Are More Than Conquerors

But if they refuse to listen to him,
  they will cross over the river of death,
dying from lack of understanding.

For the godless are full of resentment.
  Even when he punishes them,
they refuse to cry out to him for help.

They die when they are young,
  after wasting their lives in immoral living.

But by means of their suffering, he rescues those
who suffer.
  For he gets their attention through adversity.

God is leading you away from danger, Job,
  to a place free from distress.
He is setting your table with the best food.

But you are obsessed with whether the godless will
be judged.
  Don't worry, judgment and justice will be
  upheld.

But watch out, or you may be seduced by wealth.
  Don't let yourself be bribed into sin.

Could all your wealth
  or all your mighty efforts
keep you from distress?

Do not long for the cover of night,
  for that is when people will be destroyed.

Be on guard! Turn back from evil,

for God sent this suffering
to keep you from a life of evil."
  Elihu Reminds Job of God's Power

"Look, God is all-powerful.
  Who is a teacher like him?

No one can tell him what to do,
  or say to him, 'You have done wrong.'

Instead, glorify his mighty works,
  singing songs of praise.

Everyone has seen these things,
  though only from a distance.

Look, God is greater than we can understand.
  His years cannot be counted.

He draws up the water vapor
  and then distills it into rain.

The rain pours down from the clouds,
  and everyone benefits.

Who can understand the spreading of the
clouds?
and the thunder that rolls forth from heaven?

See how he spreads the lightning around him
  and how it lights up the depths of the sea.

By these mighty acts he nourishes the people,
  giving them food in abundance.

He fills his hands with lightning bolts

and hurls each at its target.

The thunder announces his presence;
the storm announces his indignant anger.

Job 31:24 New Living Translation (NLT)
"Have I put my trust in money
or felt secure because of my gold?"

Romans 5:19-21 Holman Christian Standard Bible
(HCSB)
"For just as through one man's disobedience the
many were made sinners, so also through the one
man's obedience the many will be made righ-
teous. The law came along to multiply the tres-
pass. But where sin multiplied, grace multiplied
even more so that, just as sin reigned in death,
so also grace will reign through righteousness,
resulting in eternal life through Jesus Christ our
Lord."

The law that made sin revive was more for damage
control than anything else; the law made sin live
in us now as our ruler, where we were once free to
live how we pleased. We became producers of death
and waste once sin came alive. And nothing good
happened when the law came, for it was a law made
of wrath from God.

How can the law be the good thing that we should
live by? It is the standard that God holds up, and this
law that brought sin overthrew the reigning power.
In other words, death was conquered the moment the

law was made; as God was speaking it, death was being killed. And sin now can come alive, but you now have the right and the God-given rule to have dominion over sin, where it cannot come and rule you, but you rule it. It was this law of God that made sin abound in so many ways, because we were the unrighteous people; and those that were righteous were lawless people who had no law. But the unrighteous do now, and whoever abides by the law is blessed. The law came so sin could be in abundance, but God is a Man who meets your wager and beats it. If sin was in abundance, then God abounds even more so. Thus, the verse where Jesus says, *"The thief came to steal, kill and destroy, but I came to give life and give it more abundantly."*

John 10:10 Holman Christian Standard Bible (HCSB)
"A thief comes only to steal and to kill and to destroy. I have come so that they may have life and have it in abundance."

For those of you who don't know, the devil is a thief; he is always looking to steal from you, to kill your dreams and aspirations, and to destroy your life. But do not worry, for God came to give you life—and not just life, but life in abundance. All that comes with life is more than money; it's a life that is lived in satisfaction and communion with Jesus Christ Himself—Almighty God.

You mean that God had ulterior motives? Yes, God

gave the law knowing that He is the only one to fulfill it, that the only way to have life instead of death, and to walk among His creation once again, would be in Jesus. Jesus is God—not separate, not two separate entities, but one—the one and only God, who said that He will be our salvation.

John 17:20-21 Holman Christian Standard Bible (HCSB) Jesus Prays for All Believers
"I pray not only for these, but also for those who believe in Me through their message.
May they all be one,
as You, Father, are in Me and I am in You.
May they also be one in Us,
so the world may believe You sent Me."

John 3:16 says:

 John 3:16 Holman Christian Standard Bible (HCSB) "
For God loved the world in this way: He gave His One and Only Son, so that everyone who believes in Him will not perish but have eternal life."

The law made sin still reign in death, but that is where it ended; now the grace that is given to us, that grace of God that we have access to, allows us to reign in righteousness once again. But now, the way we reign is in Jesus Christ, who brings us to eternal life.

Side note:

Jesus reigns supreme, and He has eternal life up in

heaven, right? If Jesus came down here as fully God and fully man, the man part of him died away, but the God part still remained. Now God has eternal life, so death in its purest form can't even take the everlasting life that is Jesus Christ, the Lord God, our Savior and King, because He went to hell and took the keys and shamed the devil, who was the ruler of all those who were dead before the death and resurrection of Jesus.

So, how can death take eternal life? He can't, because death has until a certain time period when it is no more. And eternal life has no time; he runs out of nothing—he made time, and death started when time was already made.

Jesus blew through the aftereffects like nothing, because how can death take eternal life? It's eternal.

Romans 8:7-9 New American Standard Bible (NASB) *"Because the mind set on the flesh is hostile toward God; for it does not subject itself to the law of God, for it is not even able to do so, and those who are in the flesh cannot please God. However, you are not in the flesh but in the Spirit, if indeed the Spirit of God dwells in you. But if anyone does not have the Spirit of Christ, he does not belong to Him."*

The mind, then, is in two forms but has one body: 1) the carnal mind, which brings death; and 2) the spiritual mind, which brings life and peace.

The carnal mind is enmity against God, because it doesn't yield to His law, so it brings death. The reason the flesh carries the carnal mind is because when the fruit was eaten it was not just a fruit, but it was the thought of an action that was taken into effect. And when the fruit was eaten, then the thought was the first carnal thought, and because the thought was of carnality, then the human mind now is based on the thoughts of carnality. And the thought you produce is the action you bring forth; thus, these are the reasons why the devil wants to occupy your mind and why you get all those thoughts you do. And the carnal mind is not one that you can change, due to the fact that it was made in death, and the mind you're born with is a mind trying to take God down and exalt yourself—kind of sounds like a vision of the devil.

Now the people that are born with this mind are the people of the flesh. This is the mind that dies away when you get baptized. That is the why in the flesh it is so hard to please God. It is not in the right mind frame—you're in the devil's mind frame, and the flesh yields to that. Sin acknowledges you as a citizen of his system, and now how can God pour out His anointing on a man when the man's mind is a citizen of sin and death and rebellion against God? He can't, and He won't give His wealth to a wicked, evil man.

The spiritual mind is life and peace with God, because this is the mind that God has given to you—a mind of peace, where worry doesn't get you; a mind where poverty has no hold on you. This is the mind that, when man decides to join God has to look over and say, "What are you doing?" because He knows that nothing is going to stop you. This is the mind that takes the limits off of God, and where faith has the liberty to do what it needs to do. This is the mind that God acknowledges—those who believe Him will be acknowledged as blessed, and the anointing of God will be upon them, and they will live a blessed life in prosperity and abundance.

Romans 8:9 New American Standard Bible (NASB) *"However, you are not in the flesh but in the Spirit, if indeed the Spirit of God dwells in you. But if anyone does not have the Spirit of Christ, he does not belong to Him."*

We that have the Holy Spirit in us are not in the flesh anymore. Nothing of us moves in the flesh. The sin that we were in made the body of the flesh move, just like now that we are in the body of Christ, what we do moves the body forward or backward. But now that we are no longer in the flesh but are in the Spirit of God, we move in a way that is contrary to popular belief. Being that this whole world made the body of death and the body of sin move in a way that was more powerful than we can imagine. Now that the Spirit of God dwells in us, we are a part of a new body that moves with God. But we must first learn how to move with God. It is a process that many people must relearn, but in all reality the way

God moves was hardwired into us and it's like riding a bike.

You may struggle a little bit, but as you go along you start moving in the way that you were originally supposed to move. You went back to basics, back to your roots, and found instantly what you were to do. You were reminded of the power that you carry, so now the few of you who are led by the Spirit of God to heal have decided to obey the Word of God, and you look back at who you are. That healing that God wanted you to bring forth was not that hard. It came forth because you obeyed and believed in what God had told you.

For it was not you, but the Spirit of God that was using you—the part of the body that had come back. You might be the finger, you might be the wrist, you might be the elbow or the knee, but you were the one who was willing to obey and listen to what God wanted you to do.

Now, everyone can say they're a Christian, but if they do not have the Spirit of God—the Holy Spirit—then they are not of God. How can they be in the body and the Spirit not fill that area up? They are not God's, then. You must know the Spirit of God so that when you see some other person, that person can't fool you, because you'll see that the same Spirit that filled you up is the same exact Spirit that fills him up. You've got to have a relationship with God in order to pick out who's a liar and a fraud, and who's a person who tells the truth.

Romans 8:10 New Living Translation (NLT)
"And Christ lives within you, so even though your body will die because of sin, the Spirit gives you life because you have been made right with God."

When the Spirit of God is in you, your body is dead—the reason why is because of sin. And when Christ comes into you, the body would die again, because Christ is in you and sin can't be where God is. And the Holy Spirit is life because of righteousness, but not your righteousness. Your righteousness is like a dirty rag, but the righteousness of God is what makes it life and is what makes us righteous.

It is through faith in God and belief in His Spirit. And when that Holy Spirit came into you, you then were made new. It was your belief in God that was accounted to you as righteousness, but when you believed God to send his Holy Spirit, and the Holy Spirit came into you, you then were made righteous through the faith of God. It is God's faith that makes us righteous in Him; it is His belief, that is carried through us back to Him, that cleans us and makes us right.

Romans 8:11 New Living Translation (NLT)
"The Spirit of God, who raised Jesus from the dead, lives in you. And just as God raised Christ Jesus from the dead, he will give life to your mortal bodies by this same Spirit living within you."

Now, if that same resurrection Spirit dwells in you that was in Christ, then you now have life in you, because you are associated with the Spirit through Jesus Christ, who is now in you. We then carry the glory that was and is in Jesus. For earlier it is written that He was raised by the glory of the Father. Now Jesus Christ is the One we died with, and the flesh we had was placed in that tomb where Jesus was laid when we were baptized with water. Since we were tied into and united in the death of His body, we should also be tied into the resurrection as well. And because the glory was on Jesus and we fused ourselves to Jesus, then the glory of the Father is then on us as well.

The same Holy Spirit that Jesus had when He was resurrected is the same exact Spirit that gives us life now. We may live because we were murdered by sin. We were once dead, but God has revived us, so we now are fruitful. And this life which He has can only be obtained through His Spirit that dwells in you. That is what brings this spiritual aspect to the physical one.

Romans 8:12 Modern English Version (MEV)
"Therefore, brothers, we are debtors not to the flesh, to live according to the flesh."

Debtor:

Function: *noun* 1)
 one guilty of neglect or violation of duty

2) one who owes a debt

So now we owe no one other than the Spirit of God, for we no longer owe a debt to the flesh. Because if we live according to the flesh, then we die, and the debt is unfulfilled. The reason why it is unfulfilled is because we live up to a debtor who is a creation of unfulfilled living. He knows nothing of completeness, then.

But live by the Spirit, and you put to death the deeds of the flesh—that means that the sins that you commit, you can kill, if you have decided to live by the Holy Spirit and live a Spirit-led life. The reason why you can now kill those sins you commit is because you no longer owe him anything; before, you were indebted to sin, so you committed the act. When you fought, you heard, "You owe me big time. Listen to me as your king or die a thousand deaths!" But now that the Spirit of God is in us we can say, "I am now complete in Christ; my debt is paid in full, and I no longer owe you anything. You are now trespassing on my property, for this land was bought with too high a price—this land belongs to God! Now get out, for I come in the name of Jesus." You put to death the deeds of the flesh now that you live according to the Spirit, because you act in His ways. You do what He says to do.

The thoughts that you have dictate the actions you bring forth. Deeds are actions you follow. If your mind is stayed on Christ, your mind may get tired, but you wait on the Lord and you renew your mind daily in His Word, because you're in the Spirit. And the Spirit then kills the sin, because the anointing is like "Raid" to sin... it kills sin on contact.

Romans 8:13 Holman Christian Standard Bible (HCSB)
"For if you live according to the flesh, you are going to die. But if by the Spirit you put to death the deeds of the body, you will live."

The flesh brings forth death; if that was the first thing to take the ground, then that is what would dominate. And life would die, because the domineering factor was death. Any life, death would take away; but the good news is that life was what made this world, and everything in it has life. The other good thing is that life, then, is the first to take the land. Then everything of death dies, because life is the dominant force there.

We are not debtors to the flesh, to live according to the flesh. We don't owe them any more—they are done, because if you do the deeds of the flesh you are done. You are dead.

We are then debtors to the Spirit, to live according to the Spirit. And it's when we live by the Spirit that sin must die, and then we live. For me now to stay alive in the Spirit of God, I must kill the deeds of the flesh.

For the Spirit of God cannot live where death also

reigns. If you're a Christian and you're still living in sin, and yet you have the Holy Spirit (somehow), then you are dead.

For you to live, you must have the Spirit of God in you now. And when you have been given life and the flesh wants to carry out its deeds, you must kill those deeds, lest you die again. Because when the Spirit of God is over you and in you, then you have the God-given authority to execute and to say "No!" to sin.

Pastor Wigglesworth gave this example of Ananias and Saphira: "They lied to God in a time of the early church revival, and it cost them their lives." Because they not only lied to God, they were spiritually extorting His movement. They were people who had the Holy Spirit and yet chose to follow the deeds of the flesh, and they lost the Holy Spirit—and when He left, they died.

Romans 8:12-17 The Message (MSG)
"So don't you see that we don't owe this old do-it-yourself life one red cent. There's nothing in it for us, nothing at all. The best thing to do is give it a decent burial and get on with your new life. God's Spirit beckons. There are things to do and places to go! This resurrection life you received from God is not a timid, grave-tending life. It's adventurously expectant, greeting God with a childlike "What's next, Papa?" God's Spirit touches our spirits and confirms who we really are. We know who he is, and

we know who we are: Father and children. And we know we are going to get what's coming to us—an unbelievable inheritance! We go through exactly what Christ goes through. If we go through the hard times with him, then we're certainly going to go through the good times with him!"

When the Spirit of God is in you and you lead a life that is Spirit-led, then you are known as a son of God. I am saying that once you start to kill sin and you live by the Spirit, then God takes you in as His son. We are then princes, for He is the true King and the only King. And Jesus then showed us what He was able to be by being a Son of God; all we have to do is believe in Jesus and have a relationship with God, and He will take us in and make us a part of His royal line. And this Holy Spirit which we connect ourselves to allowed us to receive a spirit of adoption and call out, crying, "Abba, Father!" the way you would when you see your father after a long day or a bad time at school. That is who we are bound to.

Romans 8:15-17 The Message (MSG)
"This resurrection life you received from God is not a timid, grave-tending life. It's adventurously expectant, greeting God with a childlike "What's next, Papa?" God's Spirit touches our spirits and confirms who we really are. We know who he is, and we know who we are: Father and children. And we know we are going to get what's coming to us—an unbelievable inheritance! We go through exactly

what Christ goes through. If we go through the hard times with him, then we're certainly going to go through the good times with him!"

You are in the process of being adopted as a family member in Christ; you need a witness to now say, "She is a part of the family of God." Yeah, you're here, but you need an authority figure to now finalize this agreement and to say, "I bear witness to the adoption of (whatever your name is) as a member of Jesus Christ." After this process of being saved, then you are a joint heir with Christ. You and Jesus then are brothers, family members. He will be the big brother that you can't even fathom—imagine Jesus Christ as your Big Brother. If you would just fight alongside of Him, then the glory will come later. You'll be glorified with Him by Him saying, "This is one of my siblings that fought with me, and I love them."

Romans 8:18 Holman Christian Standard Bible *(HCSB) "For I consider that the sufferings of this present time are not worth comparing with the glory that is going to be revealed to us."*

Whatever you may be going through right now, it is no match for the power of God that is in your life. There is a glory that can only come forward when you are in a test, formally known as a battle. We'll see what happens when the power of God is made manifest through us in that faith—the faith to believe in Him.

For We Are More Than Conquerors

The Word of God is much more powerful than anything that the world can bring to attack you with. The glory that is within us is much more than any attack that comes against us. The power of God moves so strongly in we that believe in Him, that there is no power in this world that can stop us from moving in the divine authority of God. The only thing that can stop you from moving in such power and authority is 1) your obedience 2) the realization that God wants to use you 3) your imagination that makes you say that you can only go up to this point in God, and then the power that He has given to you has to be capped—because that is the extent that you can go to.

The glory that is in us that came from the Father is the same glory that raised Jesus.

Romans 5:3-5 Evangelical Heritage Version (EHV)
"Not only this, but we also rejoice confidently in our sufferings, because we know that suffering produces patient endurance, and patient endurance produces tested character, and tested character produces hope. And hope will not put us to shame, because God's love has been poured out into our hearts by the Holy Spirit, who was given to us."

You will never know the power of God in your life if you don't push it to the maximum level. Push your faith to the borders and see if you can increase your faith in God by believing God.

If you're going through a time right now and don't

know what else to do, then Christ is exercising your spirit man. The glory that you have won't be extinguished by the trial you're going through. God is just bringing it forward in you, that is all, so the test that you are going through shouldn't be compared to the glory which shall be revealed in you.

Romans 8:19 New Century Version (NCV)
"Everything God made is waiting with excitement for God to show his children's glory completely."

The world that God has made is waiting for the unveiling of God's sons; His sons are the expectation of all that is in the world.

Now you're going through a time, and you think you're going to fail God—but God is bringing forth the glory He made in you. The glory of God is being made manifest in you that do believe Him. And the glory of the Father that you carry, all the world is now awaiting it to be set free—that is why you are fighting the way you are fighting. The glory of the Father that is in you sets all the captives free; it makes creation rejoice at the sound of God coming forth. It is the sound of the redeemed that cracks the chains; it's the fulfillment of Isaiah 58:7-14 and Isaiah 61:1-7.

Isaiah 58:7-14 New Living Translation (NLT)
"Share your food with the hungry,
and give shelter to the homeless.
Give clothes to those who need them,
and do not hide from relatives who need your help.

For We Are More Than Conquerors

Then your salvation will come like the dawn,
  and your wounds will quickly heal.
Your godliness will lead you forward,
  and the glory of the Lord will protect you from
  behind.

Then when you call, the Lord will answer.
  'Yes, I am here,' he will quickly reply.
Remove the heavy yoke of oppression.
  Stop pointing your finger and spreading vicious
  rumors!

Feed the hungry,
  and help those in trouble.
Then your light will shine out from the darkness,
  and the darkness around you will be as bright
  as noon

The Lord will guide you continually,
  giving you water when you are dry
and restoring your strength.
  You will be like a well-watered garden,
like an ever-flowing spring.

Some of you will rebuild the deserted ruins of
your cities.
  Then you will be known as a rebuilder of walls
and a restorer of homes.

Keep the Sabbath day holy.
  Don't pursue your own interests on that day,
but enjoy the Sabbath
  and speak of it with delight as the Lord's holy day

Honor the Sabbath in everything you do on that day,
  and don't follow your own desires or talk idly.

Then the Lord will be your delight.
  I will give you great honor
and satisfy you with the inheritance I promised to your
ancestor Jacob.
  I, the Lord, have spoken!"

Isaiah 61:1-7 New Living Translation (NLT)
  "The Spirit of the Sovereign Lord is upon me,
    for the Lord has anointed me
  to bring good news to the poor.
    He has sent me to comfort the brokenhearted
  and to proclaim that captives will be released
    and prisoners will be freed.

He has sent me to tell those who mourn
  that the time of the Lord's favor has come,
and with it, the day of God's anger against their
enemies.

To all who mourn in Israel,
  he will give a crown of beauty for ashes, a
  joyous
blessing instead of mourning,
  festive praise instead of despair.
In their righteousness, they will be like great
oaks
  that the Lord has planted for his own glory.

They will rebuild the ancient ruins,

repairing cities destroyed long ago.
They will revive them,
  though they have been deserted for many
  generations.

Foreigners will be your servants.
  They will feed your flocks
and plow your fields
  and tend your vineyards.

You will be called priests of the Lord,
  ministers of our God.
You will feed on the treasures of the nations
  and boast in their riches.

Instead of shame and dishonor,
  you will enjoy a double share of honor.
You will possess a double portion of prosperity
in your land,
  and everlasting joy will be yours."

It is the power of God that is in you that makes you more than a conqueror in Christ Jesus our Lord!

Romans 8:20-21 New Century Version (NCV)
"Everything God made was changed to become useless, not by its own wish but because God wanted it and because all along there was this hope: that everything God made would be set free from ruin to have the freedom and glory that belong to God's children."

You see, there was a forced obligation to serve death, making them servants—meaning that all creation was futile. And it was made useless because God made it a subject now of hope. Before there was no hope, there was no obligation—but now because of Him, Christ Jesus, all creation is now a subject to hope, making creation a servant.

That means that everything on this earth was a slave to death, even the family dog. But creation did not have a choice. They were now forced into this choice to live unto God, so that way they might be free from the captivity of sin and death.

And so you know that the enemy also wants the animals:

Matthew 8:30-31 New Century Version (NCV)
"Near that place there was a large herd of pigs feeding. The demons begged Jesus, 'If you make us leave these men, please send us into that herd of pigs.'"

Romans 8:22 New American Standard Bible (NASB)
"For we know that the whole creation groans and suffers the pains of childbirth together until now."

Every creation on this earth is in the middle of having birth pangs, like the lava coming forth from inactive volcanoes, or the earthquakes happening all over the world, or animals acting out of character. All of these are characteristics of things that are coming forth from death unto life.

Romans 8:23 New Century Version (NCV)
"Not only the world, but we also have been waiting

with pain inside us. We have the Spirit as the first part of God's promise. So, we are waiting for God to finish making us his own children, which means our bodies will be made free."

The Spirit of God has given us the first fruits of Himself, and He now is stirring up the spirit man inside you. And the spirit of your soul is groaning for the adoption of God to release you from the slavery of death. He may now redeem this body that makes you move in the ways of sin that hold you. You ask to be redeemed from the flesh that makes you do the deeds you do—the deeds that are an abomination to God, that is what you ask to be redeemed from.

When you ask the Lord to come into you, He then must transform everything about you, even your outward physical appearance. You must completely change your soul, mind, heart, and physical body. When God comes into you, He transfigures you into His likeness, being the very glory of God. Even this is shown when God showed up to Saul, now named Paul. And everything about Paul changed... everything. He was not the same person; this only comes to those that yield themselves to the Lord and that accept Him fully into all areas of their lives.

When the Holy Spirit comes into you, you will not want any more sin in your life. You will not act the way that you act now, which is one way at church speaking devil tongues, and then another way at the bar or at a club. Or even at home, acting as a wild person screaming at your family or saying things that are bad about your kids.

Romans 8:24,25 The Voice (VOICE)
"For we have been saved in this hope and for this future. But hope does not involve what we already have or see. For who goes around hoping for what he already has? But if we wait expectantly for things we have never seen, then we hope with true perseverance and eager anticipation."

This hope that we have been made subject to now is a hope that is shown in a different way. That hope cannot be seen yet because it is not yet here, but it is saying that it will get here at a certain time. We must believe and trust that the thing will happen; that is the same hope that we serve now. Now, would you really have to trust in something that is already here and that you don't have to believe for? That is not real hope, because it is already made manifest. Here is the difference between knowing that the object is there, and having faith and believing something is there.

The thing that you believe and wait for—that is, hope for the things not yet seen—that is the faith brought forward through your belief. When you are willing to go without the thing so that you might obtain the thing that you really want, that is perseverance through your faith.

For example: it was wintertime, and I needed a coat—the coat that I had was bad, and I needed a new one. I decided to get this nice Columbia winter jacket, and it was expensive. I needed a coat, but I waited. My parents said, "Get a different jacket for now; forget the coat." And they were going to buy me a jacket that was cheaper. I said, "I'll wait for the coat."

Before you get the breakthrough, the opportunity arises somewhere else, making you think it is better.

Two months went by of me using the same old coat. I had by this time rejected all other coats and wanted that jacket. Well, after two months I knew I was going to get the jacket, and I got it.

I had to wait two months, in the winter. And in New York it gets cold, but God gave me a new jacket that was able to last through two years, and I felt no cold.

Once you have hope, then you will eagerly wait for that thing with perseverance.

Romans 8:26-27 The Voice (VOICE)
"A similar thing happens when we pray. We are weak and do not know how to pray, so the Spirit steps in and articulates prayers for us with groaning too profound for words. Don't you know that He who pursues and explores the human heart intimately knows the Spirit's mind because He pleads to God for His saints to align their lives with the will of God?"

As you hope and persevere through your trial you become weak; because you are pushing through a trial using everything, you must maintain your strength. And that is where the Spirit of God comes in. When you pray in the Holy Ghost, He makes intercession for you in a way that can't even be spoken of.

He is the person who takes over now, when you are tired and can't go on. He is the person who, while you're fighting, prays and makes intercession for you, so you may make it through the end of this battle and receive your rewards.

And the only One who can pick up the language is the One who placed His Spirit there. God is the only One who can read the heart of man, and if the Holy Spirit was placed in your heart, the only One who can hear Him is Jesus Christ. Because it is only God that can read the heart of a man.

This also gives us a hint as to how we should pray in tongues or native languages. We should pray with our whole hearts, from our hearts to God. And when you get that real, why should He not show up and be real to you, then, as well?

And the way it works is this: now you are praying in the Spirit and the Spirit is making intercession for you, but the will of God for you has now been given to the Holy Spirit to make intercession. And you, praying in the Spirit, agree with the Holy Spirit, which has been given the information in how to make intercession for you. So in all actuality, when you pray in the Spirit you are asking that God be brought forth to God, and asking Him to intercede on your behalf from Himself. So it's God coming back to God, and you are actually coming into agreement with His Word and His will for your life.

Romans 8:28 Holman Christian Standard Bible (HCSB)
"We know that all things work together for the good of those who love God: those who are called according to His purpose."

For the people that love to do the work of God and love God and would do anything for Him, then all the things that happen in their life are good—no bad could befall them. All the so-called mishaps work together to chisel out the will of God that is in your life.

Now, if the Spirit of God is making intercession for you and you walk out the will of God in your life, then the good will of the Father is being brought into the life of the believer.

And we know now that all things work together for good for those that love God, and those that do love God are called to do His will.

You would never see a preacher that God has called to do His will ever wanting to give God up or looking at his privilege as a burden. Because of all the things that they who love God do, God makes sure that good always befalls them. So that thing and that circumstance that you have, look at it as God trying to give you a good thing. God wants to make you prosperous; He is trying to bless you, but He first has to chip you out of this ice block that you are in. And because you are fused to the ice block called death, it may hurt. But after you thaw out, you can move in that area freely.

For each of us that take God up as an adventurer, we walk in His love. We find our purpose, and those that love and have decided to walk in their purpose with God are the people who are blessed by God and have a blessed life.

Romans 8:29 New Living Translation (NLT)
"For God knew his people in advance, and he chose them to become like his Son, so that his Son would be the firstborn among many brothers and sisters."

Now in Jeremiah, God said that he knew him before he was made; he foreknew that Jeremiah was going to be born, and of his anointing and his relationship with God.

And if God knew you before you were born, then He predestined you to be *conformed* to the image of His Son.

Conform

1) to be similar or identical; *also* : to be in agreement or harmony – used with *to* or *with* <changes that *conform* with our plans>

2) a : to be obedient or compliant – usually used with *to* <*conform* to another's wishes>; b : to act in accordance with prevailing standards or customs <the pressure to *conform*>

Now, when I am born with a purpose, then I am conformed into the image of Jesus Christ. And on top of that, the love that I have for Jesus also allows me to live a life that is called good and blessed by God. And He made us into the image of the Son, Jesus, so that Christ may be the firstborn among many brothers.

We that are saved and raised by God are brothers with Him—and not any brothers, but identical twin brothers.

And those who have been made in the image of Jesus, these He called; and those who are called are justified by God, and those who are justified are glorified.

I remember when God said, *"If my people, who are called by my name, will humble themselves and pray, I will hear from heaven and heal their land."*

2 Chronicles 7:14 New King James Version (NKJV) *"If My people who are called by My name will humble themselves, and pray and seek My face, and turn from their wicked ways, then I will hear from heaven, and will forgive their sin and heal their land."*

Well, the people who are called by the name of God

are any believers who have a relationship with God. And any believer who has a relationship with God, He calls for His purpose. And if you are called and humble yourself and pray, then God will heal your land, which is your soul.

And if anybody says anything, you have been justified, and *justified* means:

Justified

1) a : to prove or show to be just, right, or reasonable; b (1) : to show to have had a sufficient legal reason; (2) : to qualify (oneself) as a surety by taking oath to the ownership of sufficient property

2) a : *archaic* : to administer justice to; b : *archaic* : ABSOLVE; c : to judge, regard, or treat as righteous and worthy of salvation

3) a : to space (as lines of text) so that the lines come out even at the margin; b : to make even by justifying <*justified* margins>
intransitive verb

1) a : to show a sufficient lawful reason for an act done; b : to qualify as bail or surety

2) to justify lines of text
synonym: see MAINTAIN

You have enough lawful reason for acting the way you're acting, because it is not you who are acting, but the Spirit of God acting through you. You see, I am not doing anything myself, but I do what I see my Father in heaven doing. God is healing the sick, so Jesus healed the sick, so I can heal the sick. God raised the dead, so Jesus raised the dead, so I can raise the dead, in the name of Jesus.

Romans 8:31-32 The Voice (VOICE)
"So what should we say about all of this? If God is on our side, then tell me: whom should we fear? If He did not spare His own Son, but handed Him over on our account, then don't you think that He will graciously give us all things with Him?"

If God is on our side, then what can stay in our way—what can keep us from going on strong? If God didn't even hold back His own Son for us, then how can He not give Him, and us, all things? Then if God gave His Son, why won't God give us all things?

Once God is on our side, nothing can stop us—for we have a blessing covenant with God. Our faith in God is what is counted as righteousness, and there is nothing that can govern you but God. You are also adopted into the royal, divine, and loving family of God, where He has even taken you out of slavery and killed your enemy as if it were His enemy.

So now if God is on our side as our Companion and Friend and Father, then what can possibly stop us from living an abundant life? Paul says that He even gave His only Son freely for us. So why won't God give us all things, then? If I don't have it, and God didn't give it to me, then in all reality, I don't want it.

Romans 8:33-34 New Living Translation (NLT)
"Who dares accuse us whom God has chosen for his
own? No one—for God himself has given us right
standing with himself. Who then will condemn us?
No one—for Christ Jesus died for us and was raised
to life for us, and he is sitting in the place of honor
at God's right hand, pleading for us."

Now, who can bring a charge against those who God
chose to put in there? It is God who justifies the
actions that are being done in that office, then.

If someone accuses me, then God says, "Dismissed.
I vouch for the man; I told him to do what he is
doing."

Who is going to condemn me if it was Christ who
kept me from condemnation? It was Christ, when He
died and was risen, who sits at the right hand of God
and makes intercession for us. When you sin the
way you do, it is Christ who says, "I was down there
in that situation, and it was hard for Me—so how
much more for him? Won't it be harder for him?
Forgive him; he doesn't see the consequences. And
My blood covers him."

If I am accused, God has justified; if condemned,
God has forgiven. So nothing then can stop me,
when I am in alignment with the Word of God in my
life and the Word taught to me through the teaching
of Jesus Christ. Jesus builds me up when I am in an

area for demolition.

It is always in an area of demolition that God shows up and decides to build you up there, so that way you can really stick out and shine with the light of God and show forth your praises unto a holy God.

And He shows what a master craftsman can really do when you decide to wait on God and let Him build you up.

Romans 8:35 New Living Translation (NLT)
"Can anything ever separate us from Christ's love? Does it mean he no longer loves us if we have trouble or calamity, or are persecuted, or hungry, or destitute, or in danger, or threatened with death?"

Who is going to separate us from the love of God? What can possibly keep a man from the true desire of his love? *"Shall tribulation, or distress, or persecution, or famine, or nakedness, or peril, or sword?"* Because if I remember, He says earlier that we glory in tribulation, and God can now show up in the time of your trial, as the scriptures state.

Romans 8:36 Holman Christian Standard Bible (HCSB)
"As it is written: Because of You we are being put to death all day long; we are counted as sheep to be slaughtered."

Even if we do die, we still live; we are going to get killed. Our purpose is to live, and yet it is also to die. For we that were called by God to live are His sheep, and in this life we must face those things—those persecutions. We are sheep that are accounted for the slaughter. That means that God knows how many people must die for the saving glory of God, yet count it all joy.

For I will be a living sacrifice. I fight for the Gospel of God, but if I die then let my life be a sweet smell unto my Savior and Lord.

Romans 8:37 New American Standard Bible (NASB)
"But in all these things we overwhelmingly conquer through Him who loved us."

For in these times of *"tribulation, or distress, or persecution, or famine, or nakedness, or peril, or sword"* we are more than conquerors through Him who loved us. Through the very heart of all those areas of pain, we have still conquered these things and then some. Because we are more than a conqueror, we are not only blessed in the blessing of Abraham, we are the rulers of our land—but still subject to our Lord Jesus Christ. We have the righteousness of our faith, we have the whole land that God wants us to possess, and much more.

No words can describe the power I walk with, the authority I carry, and the strength I carry, because I live through Him. And if I die, I die making the glory of God come forth through even more people. The anointing I carry has never been seen, yet the peace I have passes all understanding, and the joy

I have can never be taken away. For I have been transformed into the likeness of my Father, and what I do I have seen Him do. I walk in the divine favor of my Lord, and I bring with me the Word of God's movement. I come for mercy, I come for angels, I come for healing, I come for freedom, I come in the name of the Lord.

There is a way for a man and a woman to live before God Almighty, but in order for you to attain that level of freedom, you must work out the other areas that He tells you to work out. We must be set free from our past, for if we are to get into our future there can be nothing holding us back, tying us down from the path that God has set before us to walk out. There are grudges that are put in place that can eternally harm you and can keep you from reaching the level that God has set for you to reach. It is important for us to let go of the pain and confess to God our sins, if we are to have total healing in our lives. There are many people who talk about the goodness of God and the healing power of God, and how if you just follow through in the Word of God then He will bless you. There is more to this than we think. If we want the total healing power of God in our lives, then we must forgive and ask for total healing in our lives. God does not want you to minister to the sick in body if you are holding a grudge and won't forgive; it is impossible to move in the complete work of God in our lives, then. There is power in your words; if you were to speak the Word of God and ask for healing in the area that it is hard for you to receive healing in, it will take place (but you can't be religious). If you believe in what you say and trust God, even if you don't like it, He will heal your land.

For us to be living as more than a conqueror, we must be forgiven. If we repent from what we have done as a nation, and as a church, and as an individual in Christ, revival will break out and light will shine forth to such a degree that nothing will hold us back from the promises of God taking place in our lives. If we truly love God and enter the repentance that He is calling us into, we can finally move from the revival that we always wanted and move into the reformation that God has for us. The truth that we need is not here, based on words or ideas or what we think. If we as a people were to repent and ask God for healing in our lives, and to tear down the pride that is keeping us from the revival that we want to see come, the true Word of God would break forth in a way that we never thought possible. This is the hardest thing for us, as Christians and as a people after God's own heart, to do—for we have to admit that we were wrong in our ideology and have misrepresented what the Holy Spirit is trying to do in our lives. If we as a people repent, there is a revival coming that will knock out the people who do not want to admit that they're wrong. And when it comes time for them to move into the work of God, they will not be allowed in to see the movement that

He is bringing forth.

This is the way of being more than a conqueror—by submission to the Word of God. The Word of God in our lives depends on how we decide to listen. If we would stop refusing the Word of God in our lives, and if we would stop refusing the Holy Spirit to move the way He wants to and just listen and pay attention to what He says, nothing would stop us. The work that God wants us to do is a mighty work, but it can only take place if we as a people stop pointing fingers at each other and repent from our own wrongdoings.

God showed me something like this: I see a balloon, the type you see at the Macy's Thanksgiving Day parade. And the balloon is getting ready to go higher, but because it is tied down it can only go to a certain point. It is held down by ropes that are tied to bolts on the floor, and the balloon rips the bolts off the floor and it floats a little higher—but not as high as it can go. The bolts used to keep the balloon down have now turned into weights.

I completed *For We Are More Than Conquerors* on September 23, 2006. I started it on January 1, 2006.

In doing this study, I had to go through sleepless nights and spiritual battles in a way that I have not yet fought until now. *More Than Conquerors* was not going to go farther than twenty pages—I was fighting too hard and was going to give it up—but I had to continue, especially when I hit the area of sin. That was where the battle was big. I was about to give up, and it was like I was uncovering the weakness and the source of where he comes from. And then God said to me, "You are fighting sin itself now. I killed sin, but this is the sin that you were born into as a baby." And the sin was hard, because it hit me in the areas of weakness that I would fall into. I had done a lot of repentance in the whole study of *For We Are More Than Conquerors.*

It was hard as I went to the scriptures in Romans; as I got there I was really fighting, but every time I fought, a part of me changed. Meaning I once was acting in a way that was okay, but after doing that section of the study my whole action changed for the better. As I was in prayer, I would pray one way thinking it was okay, but as I continued, I felt like my prayer was routine. But I didn't know what it was, so after I would read and realize what I was capable of I would pray in the way that I now realized, and according to the power that was given me by God. And I knew that it was in effect, but I hadn't heard a thing or felt a thing. But I had to learn that He is not a feeling, and that is what made it very hard for me. But I was able to walk in the authority of God.

I was reading Pastor Wigglesworth's *Ever-Increasing Faith* online, and it helped me in my study. I kept on reading the chapters in Romans and praying, and I was starting to walk in the authority of the Holy Spirit. And God helped me and my family get out of many, many jams in health and in financial problems.

Upon the completion of *More Than Conquerors,* I knew that there was a way that God wanted me to live. And after hearing what God wanted for me, it made me get close in a way that I never thought I would. I still have to fight, but I know now that I can make it through. God gave me the strength to fight my flesh. He broke me out of the cycle of sin that once was upon me. When everybody said, "It's all right; don't worry about it," I asked God to break this cycle and execute this thing. And after many months of fighting and repentance, it was broken— and now I feel like the pressure is off of me and I can live as a free man, fully alive in Christ.

-Luke Soto

For We Are More Than Conquerors
Epilogue

May God strike you with His lightning and hit you at your very core, that you may go forth with the power of God, fully energized in His Spirit, and live your best life for God's glory.

May God's lightning dance across the land and cut the darkness of this current age and the age to come; may God show forth His glory, and may His fire burn in the hearts of all who believe; may that fire never go out but be passed on for future generations, and may it increase.

Love of God, go forth and show us how to love; teach us how to love Your way. For You say that perfect love casts out all fear; remove the fear we live in, in this current day and in the days to come, by giving us an inexhaustible supply that runneth over of Your love—love for the humanity that You made. Help us to live, to fight, to love our families the way You taught those of old.

We come before You asking You to show us how to fight the darkness of this age. Show us how to live, love, and worship the way You desire your people to bring You worship.

May Your blood wash over us. And forgive us. And God, it's going to have to be a supernatural thing, but help us to forgive those who have hurt us. Because honestly, I can't.

In the name of Jesus, amen.

Luke Soto
How can I be saved?

I know that this is a book for the Christian believer and for the new Christian who has just become a believer. Welcome to the life that Christ has for you. Let me just say this… it's going to be hell, because you're now coming out of the bad habits that you had before Christ grabbed you out of the hellhole you were in.

So, if you are still reading this book, and you don't know how to get out of the cycle of sin you may be living in…

Say this:

"Lord! Save me! I'm sorry—I repent and I regret my sins. I don't know any other way! Save my life and make no tarry! I accept you into my heart! Save me, because I'm scared and I don't want to die without You!"

Jeremiah 33:3 New American Standard Bible (NASB) *"Call to Me and I will answer you, and I will tell you great and mighty things, which you do not know."*

Jeremiah 33:3 New Century Version (NCV) *"Judah, pray to me, and I will answer you. I will tell you important secrets you have never heard before."*

Then, get to the nearest church you can and talk to a preacher or a priest on how to become a Christian.

Hi, so I'm Luke—I was born and raised in church. Yes, that's right—I have been saved all my life; in fact, I was the guy who sat in the row just heating up a seat and sleeping through the services.

I grew up with fire and brimstone preaching. I grew up challenging what the other Christian kids said, just because I could. I really didn't give a rip who or what this 90s "Jesus love" movement was, and honestly, I didn't care. I was into being what a kid was—then as a teen, God got ahold of this boy. As I sat in the service, I saw the power of God move in the sanctuary, and I was enamored. It woke me up to a side I had thought was dead. I saw God heal a cancer patient right there in church, and then I saw those who didn't even go up to the altar get healed just by believing God, and living the Christian life, and hearing the Word of God. Pastor Demola, thanks for living the life of Christ. You woke this boy up to the glory of God. It was God who moved, folks, not the pastor—God used the preacher just like He wants to use you. Will you let Him?

I have traveled to many churches since then, but God was always on my mind. I was always hearing from certain churches that God can't use you unless you're broken—like if you've been saved all your life, then you're not living your best life. Then God showed up and said, "Hey there, I have been waiting to meet you—I'm the Holy Spirit," and it has been a ride ever since. There were a lot of things I went through as I came closer to our Lord, and after a while He brought me to the Catholic church. And I must say that I received much healing in my soul, and I received a closer relationship with God.

I don't hold myself up as some high and mighty guy. Follow God, go read the Bible, talk to God. I did, and He made me who I am. I currently work in a hospital as a CNA, and I'm going into the nursing field. I hope you don't give up on God—He hasn't given up on you. Nothing about me is too great and grand; if you want great and grand, look to God. Me, I'm just some Christian who God taught a really cool thing: the Lord of Hosts is a fighter who loves deep and hard. So, look to Christ, not to me.

If you can't say God's name, you keep trying—the persistent get the answers.

So about me: work, school, confession, worship, prayer, eating, exploring, sleeping.

The one thing I can share with you from God is this: Do not be afraid! Boys and girls, be not afraid!

Freedom in God is possible. Be not afraid; call on God. He will save. I tell you this, as I know that God is the Lord of angel armies. By the blood that surges through Christ's body, I know that we can live a life whole and free and able to worship God. Be not afraid!

-Luke Sotot

For We Are More Than Conquerors
References

References / copyright page Merriam-Webster dictionary online © 2020 Merriam-Webster, Incorporated https://www.merriam-webster.com/

Ever Increasing Faith by Smith Wigglesworth, copyright 2016 GodSounds, Inc., all rights reserved ISBN: 1537700227 ISBN-13: 978-1537700229

Taken from THE JESUS BOOK - The Bible in Worldwide English. Copyright SOON Educational Publications, Derby DE65 6BN, UK. Used by permission.

Scripture quotations are from the Holy Bible, Evangelical Heritage Version® (EHV®) © 2019 Wartburg Project, Inc. All rights reserved. Used by permission.

Scripture quotations marked NLV are taken from the New Life Version, copyright © 1969 and 2003. Used by permission of Barbour Publishing, Inc., Uhrichsville, Ohio 44683. All rights reserved.

Scripture quotations marked HCSB are taken from the Holman Christian Standard Bible®, Copyright © 1999, 2000, 2002, 2003, 2009 by Holman Bible Publishers. Used by permission. Holman Christian Standard Bible®, Holman CSB®, and HCSB® are federally registered trademarks of Holman Bible Publishers.

Scripture taken from the New Century Version®.

Notes

_____
_____
_____
_____
_____
_____
_____
_____
_____
_____
_____
_____
_____
_____
_____
_____
_____
_____
_____
_____
_____
_____
_____
_____
_____
_____
_____
_____
_____

For We Are More Than Conquerors

Luke Soto

CPSIA information can be obtained
at www.ICGtesting.com
Printed in the USA
LVHW010155260820
664159LV00015B/1138